PADDLE ADVENTURING
with Canoe & Kayak

HERB KLINGER

Trafford
PUBLISHING

Order this book online at www.trafford.com
or email orders@trafford.com

Most Trafford titles are also available at major online book retailers.

Printed in the United States of America.

ISBN: 978-1-4251-1566-1 (sc)

Trafford rev. 11/07/2013

North America & international
toll-free: 1 888 232 4444 (USA & Canada)
fax: 812 355 4082

Dedication

For my kids, Greg and Laurie,
Their kids,
You, and yours,

and

For Judy,
My lifelong,
Always loving and giving,
Absolutely favorite paddler.

Acknowledgments

My most hearty thanks to every single paddling companion, there have been many, and not a bad apple in the bunch.

Thanks also to those who tolerated not only me but my camera. You'll be pleased to note all really embarrassing pix have been removed. Where names have come and gone, I cherish the memories, and it is my hope that this effort properly honors them. Photos by Herb; those of Herb and a number of others by Judy, and for the three of the family I thank Jim Flosdorf, Bob Johnstone, and Gordy Lomax; Dan Murphy for the cabin interior; and Greg Klinger for his illustrations and cover work.

There are many kinds of paddling, and paddlers, but all share a common affinity which includes a love of the out-of-doors, selfless comradeship, and pleasure in going beyond. Paddlers, whatever their personality, are never boring.

Last, but hardly least, I'm grateful for my steadies – a wonderful wife, Judy, who sustained our enthusiasm for the project after getting it out of the closet, and two spunky kids, Gregory and Laurie, now parents themselves, who have continued paddling with their spouses and our grandchildren.

CONTENTS

Most books on this subject fall into two categories: *How-to's* and *Grand Expeditions*. PADDLE ADVENTURING comes between those two worthy activities.

Millions of us are beneficiaries of a vast array of new outdoor and on-the-water possibilities. This fastest growing sport offers more than a lifetime of easily pursued adventures from mild to wild, from global in scope to after work, and right around home. Paddling is a universal activity unrestricted by age or sex that almost anyone can do, a recreational style that is simple, versatile, hip, wholesome, ecologically friendly, affordable, a door to freedom, connecting with nature and providing easy access to varieties of adventuring.

Increasingly we need outlets which offer diversion and simplicity in the face of daily complexity. Recent announcements touting hundreds of planned "You Can Paddle" events in the United States put it this way: "Paddling brings sanity to an insane world. It quiets society's noise and reconnects us to something vital and real. Paddling can change your life if you let it."....Chevy Trucks. James Raffan, author of Bark, Skin and Cedar, has written "To paddle a canoe is to embark on a liminal journey that can sweep a willing heart across thresholds of new worlds."

Selecting a title for this book included consideration of "IF YOU'RE A KAYAKER OR CANOEIST YOU'LL LOVE THIS BOOK." A bit too obvious, eh? So how 'bout "THE NAKED CANOEIST AND OTHER INSPIRATIONAL TALES"? Too risqué, even for some paddlers. "A PADDLER'S ECLECTIC RETROSPECTIVE COLLECTIVE"...Too cute. "A PADDLER'S HANDLE ON THE WORLD"? Too pretentious. "DIPS AND SWIRLS"? Too ethereal. "RIPPLES AND DRIPS"? Some might take that personally. "GO PADDLE"? Paddle who? "A KALEIDOSCOPIC TREASURE OF CANOE AND KAYAKING PLEASURE"? Get real. Okay, so we're at "PADDLE ADVENTURING ----WITH CANOE AND KAYAK"

PADDLE ADVENTURING is opticentric; lots of photos, saving, in theory at least, thousands of words. As for the "kaleidoscopic" mix, the versifications might sometimes conjure faint company with Rap or Cowboy Poetry, but inspired this time by the rhythm of paddle strokes, the gentle rise and fall of ocean swells, and the windy-day lapping of waves. It is an appreciation of shared experience, a window on a segment of the paddling world. Old timers, I would hope, may nod and chuckle; I wish newcomers might be encouraged to just get out there, and go.

Billy Collins, recent Poet Laureate, tells us that verse must be hospitable, easy to read, plain spoken, and with understandable humor. This, in most cases, I've tried, but, poetry police take note, I make no claim to be a poet – a versifier perhaps, and I fight down a goodly number of ditties – but not all.

Mainly I wish to share my passion for this satisfying multifaceted, multidimensional activity. There are references to much that is happening in the paddling universe – motherships, urban paddling, canoe design, canoe trails, kayak trends, paddling seniors, remedial paddling, safety, conservation, saving and restoring rivers – and some how-to's via the not-how-to's.

Here are from a variety of trips and incidents, reflections of many happy days and an invitation to anyone not yet on the water to grab a paddle.

Within each specialized aspect of the paddling world are outstanding leaders with expertise far greater than mine. Still I believe this broadly cast, eclectic, sometimes serious, often lighthearted book also validates and encourages. The title itself, PADDLE ADVENTURING, can easily conjure up images of heroic exploits. Here there are none ...but adventures, yes.

That's the whole point. Is there any so-called sport, outside of hiking-trekking-climbing-skiing perhaps, that offers a greater variety of ways to get a kick out of life? Canoeing and kayaking, once basic to survival and exploring, have burst upon the scene as another great way to liven up our modern lives. From a small boat you take out after supper, or put on the car for a weekend outing, to the longer planned vacation, that craft is your ticket to new experience, and every paddle forth, every venturing trip out, is adventuring.

Adventure is everywhere, waiting to be exposed. Adventuring is every connection to what's new. Adventure is where you find it, a personal journey to the unexpected, and for some of you I hope here. Paul Theroux in <u>Sunrise with Seamonsters</u> tells us, "I never tried to explain my trip to anyone....When I discovered that things were different out here, and unrelated to life on land, I decided to keep it a secret."

I've tried here to shed a bit of light on that "secret". The paddle offers a return to a conscious sense of body and self. From imagining to doing. Grabbing hold, a handle on your world, "paddling your own canoe"...or kayak...instantly and tangibly responsive. Buoyant. Real. Exciting. Revitalizing.

The Paddle Thing

It helped put food on aborigine tables. Then it opened up the continent. But the paddle today...an obsolete tool for grunts? Or your golden key to never imagined dimensions, discoveries, connections and....passions!

Glide into the inaccessible revealed...a hidden cove. Drift with sparkling-flowing streams. Float suspended above teeming aquaria. Dig and swivel-hip, shout and cheer downhill through surging whitewater. Or tap rhythmic strokes across liquid glass, reflecting and transcending.

Further afield, a single paddle, silently sculled, lets us join the world of the beaver, otter, and loon families. With a double, amid salt air and undulating kelp, periscoping seals follow in your wake. Passing sea lions grunt a surprised "Hello", and swim on in formation. Scrounging shoreline bears share the scene with mink, orca and magnificent breaching humpback whales. Other wildlife may include spirited fellow paddlers.

On a tropical rainforest river, sometimes running underground, experience howler monkeys and Mayan caves with their sacrificial bones and pottery. Traveling cay to cay, tradewind-filled sails convert the paddle to rudder.

Closer to home, active streams and rivers. Endless strings of lakes. Exploding monster bass. The incense and glow of campfires. Freedom, friendship, family, fellowship, shared ecstacies...tired muscles, delicious sleep; fresh coffee, new horizons.

What is paddling but arms and blade as art, science and sheer joy? Kayak and canoe brings us as close as we may ever come to the epiphany of space travel....inner and outer. The paddle, our extension into the elements, enables with solid sensuous grip, easy strokes as natural as walking, but sometimes faster. Like jogging? More like ballet.

Paddlers let ultimate destinations evolve from the going. With a simple forward stroke, the paddle activates curiosity, adventure, future. Stretching. muscles in synch, marvelous ideas have been known to pop up with the bubbles in those paddle swirls. Fresh discoveries can trigger profundities, or just an obvious answer to something that's been bugging you for weeks. By propelling body we transport the mind, free up the soul, in the process exposing aspects of the Great Soul. A Zen-like rhythm can set one ablaze with insight....and perhaps resolve. Fired by the promise of a new day, we come to know a buoyancy of fulfillment. And always the primal pleasure of fluidity in motion.

No matter where, how or why, the paddle can be a handle on the world, addictive, deeply satisfying, and all-out fun.

Paddle Adventuring

Paddle adventuring for 99.9% of us doesn't require canoeing over waterfalls or kayaking between ice floes, bashing headlong down Himalayan gorges, or rowing the Grand Canyon backwards in pursuit of a new record. It's not about knocking off the longest, fastest, mostest, highest, hairiest extremes or challenges to survival.

Rather it's following our curiosity to what's around the corner and over the horizon. It's being wide-eyed, open-minded and heartfelt from the easily reached water world around us to out and beyond. It might be as simple as creatively seeking out and finding your own quiet eddies. Or getting beyond the seduction and emptiness of commercial entertainment in favor of some old-fashioned recreation –the kind that's big as life, with spirit unleashed, and nourishing to the soul. And, for most of us, it can be close to home – with wider prospects unending.

Paddling, body and soul, is just about your easiest access to multifaceted adventure. Starting skills come naturally, at any age, along or with companions. You may capture the glory of a sky-filling sunrise....drift silently observing on a flowing stream...revel in the challenge of whitewater or coastal touring, or maybe in the growing skills of your family negotiating their way down river on a nearby outing. Grabbing a paddle also gets you to places beyond the ordinary that are only reachable by stroking your way there.

No matter from where you push off, it's never the same as last time. Adventuring comes not just from the variety of paddle-able locations, but changing conditions and what you each time bring to it – interests, yes, and always your changing, sometimes deeper needs. A short list would include physical conditioning, meditation and transcendence, cruising, competition (self included), plus a myriad of interests from fishing, sketching, photography, birding and wildlife, social outings...or all of the above. The adventure itself goes far beyond cruising or whitewater thrills. An inspirational setting or just a change of scene can trigger "inner explorations".

Webster's definition of adventure is "a stirring experience". Let's see, we stir a lot of water, heading out, striking forth, indulging questions, escaping the familiar, seeking physical release or silence and serenity....accepting, dealing with and perhaps reveling in the unexpected...going somewhere new, probing unknowns...pushing previous limits...trying fresh approaches, another point of view...challenging...exploring...in quest...doing the same thing differently...reminiscing, seeking through another's eyes..."What if?" versus "probably not", or "maybe" or "yes!"...digging "new holes" instead of the old ones deeper...opening new directions...pushing "outside the box"...kicking into high gear..."curiouser and curiouser"...Spicing up the here and now...Stretching body and soul...implementing dreams....Alive!

Paddling is a briskly growing, but not crowded sport, and it's doable from your first day out. There's water for canoes and kayaks almost everywhere, from serene mirror calm to rushing, from neighboring to tidal, to rivers, lakes and islands without names or people. Equipment, initially or on the road, rentable, is not expensive. Trying out different models of craft allows one to choose what most excites.

And now, even the outdoor retail giants are making it easier to get started. Inexpensive classes and courses are offered by R.E.I., E.M.S., and L.L. Bean, in addition to local offerings.

Sound like a self-help book? Well, yes, and perhaps more useful than most. "Shall we put in the movie, or take out the canoe?" There's one answer if you value those magical times of paddling alone or together (and starring in your own flick!)

Is paddle adventuring dangerous, life-threatening? No, just routine-threatening. When it comes to safety, we prepare for the unpredictables. But beyond that, the unpredictables are gloriously what it's all about. Welcome to a paddling universe of inexhaustible possibilities.

To be reminded of what's really great about paddling, look no further than the ads for a wide variety of major products.

Interest in canoeing and kayaking has exploded. The paddling universe has become a cultural icon. Paddlers, not the target but the beautiful bait, have arrived as admired types for promotions of everything from cosmetic to staying upright in rough financial seas.

Enjoy it: Diet Coke, with two portaging kayakers, reminds us that "AS SEEN ON TV IS NOT YOUR STYLE". And Royal Caribbean's kayaking couple implores us, "LET EVERYTHING GO BUT THE PADDLE."

A "how you spend your time" ad tells us..."LIVE TO RIDE THE CREST. SPRAY FLYING."; and so rides that paddling essential, an Esquire watch. Not to be outdone, in a double page ad, Timex has a canoeing couple with "DEAR DIARY, THERE ARE NO WORDS FOR THIS."

Three kayakers on a windy lake illustrate "THE ROAD TO DISCOVERY...WHERE THE VIEW IS ALWAYS CHANGING...THE ADVENTURE ALWAYS NEW.", leading us to Hyatt's web site, "YOUR PASSAGE TO THE WORLD." Two double-kayakers, promoting New Zealand, advise us to "DISCOVER RATHER THAN ESCAPE." Chubb has a couple in a canoe watching the sunrise with "HOW TO PRESERVE A MEMORY." North Carolina's sunset kayaker is in "A BETTER PLACE TO BE."

Smiling gamely as he struggles, a rapids-running guide assures us "EVERYBODY NEEDS TO GET OUT OCCASIONALLY", and in addition to "Toothbrush, clean undies", there's Yahoo!Mobile, from "ANY STRANGE PLACE YOU WANT TO WANDER."

Standing tall with dripping paddles before a docked canoe, we admire her beaming face, courtesy of Wilmington Trust: "RECOGNIZING WORTH"..."THERE IS NO ONE LIKE YOU...YOU ARE ONE IN SIX BILLION", and who wouldn't mind making it two in six billion, with another turn around the lake?

A lone kayaker drifting calmly in Glacier Bay is proclaimed "inspected by expert #34, proffered by iExplore, which echoes an expression wives have been known to use: "COME BACK DIFFERENT!"

Hard to ignore, that caressable wooden canoe under "THE BEST THINGS IN LIFE ARE BASIC", sporting a pack of cigarettes on its elegantly caned seat. "MORE PLACES TO EXPLORE" takes a solo paddler straight to Woolrich. An obviously determined young female kayaker needs "someone who can HELP ME LOOK OUT FOR MYSELF" as she aims for the Lincoln Financial Group. T. Rowe Price poses a grinning retired couple canoeing for "NOTHING LASTS FOREVER, but your retirement income can last a lifetime." GTE's formally dressed pair, whitewater kayaking, his tie flying, struggles in behalf of "SERVICES WITHOUT SINKING THE BOAT...". AFLAC Inc. has "an INTREPID BOATMAN", a " DAUNTLESS FELLOW navigating today's hazardous economy" while they, equally heroic, are "the ones who float Wall Street's boat". And then, don't be distracted, but "WHAT CAN CLASS 5 RAPIDS TEACH US ABOUT MANAGING WEALTH?"

When is a paddle more powerful than a shotgun? When Ducks Unlimited quotes Aldo Leopold: "WHEN WE SEE LAND AS A COMMUNITY TO WHICH WE BELONG, WE MAY BEGIN TO USE IT WITH LOVE AND RESPECT", the ad illustrated by a solitary paddle-wielding canoeist...and nary a duck blind.

A bit of a stretch, perhaps, is the full-page canoeing close-up for Estee Lauder's Resilience Eye Cream. But, be assured, it's "ULTRA-HYDRATING" and, beyond a smile that melts, she's holding her paddle correctly.

Paddling variety further includes "SURVIVE THE UNBELIEVABLE" in an unbelievable craft (Rubbermaid); "IT'S ABOUT MAKING EVERY MOMENT COUNT" (Advantage/10); and that fellow reading his newspaper in a heritage canoe placed comfortably on the grass, is there for "Go RVing. LIFE'S A TRIP." A *News week* article has an overworked, wired guy kayaking in his office.

With few exceptions and an occasional stretch, these messages do manage to relate. That couple floating into a sunset for Cafe Vienna under the slogan "DRIFT PURPOSELY THROUGH LIFE" does speak to me. But I would want my kids to know "You gotta know when to paddle." Meanwhile, Marathon in the Florida Keys wants us to "PADDLE YOUR KIDS AND THEY'LL LOVE YOU FOR IT."

Then there are the TV commercials exuding on-the-water excitement or paddlers saturated in sunsets. They make me want to drop what I'm doing to run right out and buy....more time to paddle.

Whatever these ads do for their products, they are paddlesport supportive. They may be our hitchhikers but they are also, in this often hectic, efficiency-driven, consumer-oriented, time-conscious, technologically-focused age, a compliment to our values. Pangs of nostalgia rise when looking at USAA 's family portaging scene, encouraging us to "FOCUS ON THE IMPORTANT THINGS". Portaging was a very important travel component for our little ones, plodding with plucky devotion, and ....believe it...occasional groans but no complaints. They understood effort as necessary and natural to each next goal. What a great lesson learned early!

And what a formula these ads – You, your love, a canoe, a kayak, a sunset...your reverie...and zap!...the product. Oh, well, thank$ for the reverie$.

Better yet, you get a chance to stroke on..."HEAR YOURSELF THINK", "YOUR DREAMS COME TRUE" "RESTART YOUR ENGINE", "PADDLE TOGETHER", "JUST ADD WATER", "THE EMOTION OF MOTION", "UNPLUG", "RAPID HEARTBEAT", "SUNSHINE ON SALE", "RIDING HIGH"...."THE SPIRITED TRADITION", "LET YOUR DREAMS DO THE CHASING", "NEW LIFT, NEW LIFE", and we all cheer this one, "EXPECT OUTSTANDING LIQUIDITY."....so   "Smile, stroke, celebrity bloke,

You're the new model for insurance to Coke.

Our craft once thought of as yachts for the poor,

Now glow with allure, sure to sell more and more.

O.K., Beautiful People. Catch Advantage/10, which has you drifting on a misty morning..."It's about making every moment count"..."TASTE LIFE.".

Yes!!! Those are the ads. *You're the reality.*

HERITAGE

In the interior they paddled bark, held together with roots and sap.

Our computer-designed craft are made of Kevlar, Thionyl, and Nitrosylus.

On the coast they went for whales in seal skin stretched over driftwood....

or in a hollowed-out tree.

Aleut baidarkas – kayaks– in pursuit of the otter, traveled from their Arctic homes as far south as San Francisco.

We can sit in our tough, watertight kayaks,
with foam seats, booties, and gloves, Gore–tex.
A wet suit even.....**What did they wear?**
We're fueled with three squares, with
carefully measured vitamins and minerals, with
power bars and beverages to balance our electrolytes...
What did they eat?
Could they imagine a back country canoeist
with GPS? Weather radio? Cell phone? ....
Electrically warmed socks? Constantly sipping from
a plastic water bottle "to prevent dehydration"?

They paddled harder,
And probably smarter,
Their skill begged survival.

The ancestors of these Hudson Bay freighters were large fur-bearing 32' to 40' HBC and Montreal canoes. They could carry eight tons and were the first linking, binding entity of what we today know as Canada.

Hudson Bay operations began in 1607 here in Moose Factory. By the 1820's, in amalgamation with the pioneering French, HBC ruled all northern waterways coast to coast.

The canoe – vehicle to an empire – gift of the Native peoples. In return....the motor.

FIRST NATIONS PADDLERS, HERE FROM
OREGON TO ALASKA AND THE
NORTHWEST TERRITORIES......

IN THEIR ARTFULLY DESIGNED
AND CONSTRUCTED TRADITIONAL
CANOES......

ONCE AGAIN COME TOGETHER, SHARING A PROUD HERITAGE..........

**FILLING THIS HARBOUR
AFTER A CENTURY'S
ABSENCE.
VICTORIA, B.C.**

Kayaking in Europe? That is where this folding kayak originated, over a century ago when a German tailor designed a boat he could knapsack to his put-ins by train. The Klepper enabled one to paddle anywhere. Today's technology has created all manner of sleek light collapsibles, empowering all-season, global possibilities. Tonga, anyone? Galapagos?

Paddling the Pacific? Outrigger canoes connected and populated the islands. In recent times Paul Theroux's odyssey with folding Klepper is described in his book, *The Happy Isles of Oceania: Paddling the Pacific.*

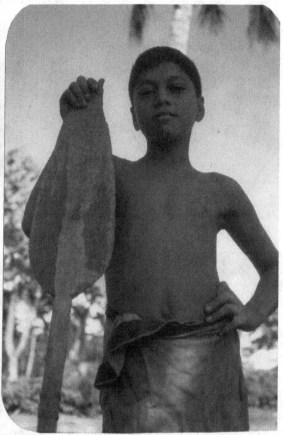

PROUD TO

PADDLE

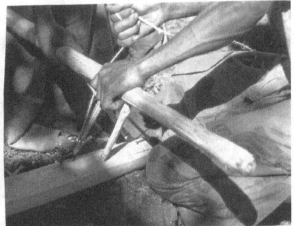

WESTERN SAMOA

THAILAND

ZAIRE

Dugouts continue to serve all over Sub-Sahara Africa, in the rain forests of South America, and among the boat people on the rivers of Southeast Asia. Although the working paddle has increasingly given way to the Yamaha, especially with the larger boats, most river dwellers still skillfully zip around with paddle and pole. Motors are not only beyond their means, but not necessarily useful to their traditional ways.

CONGO RIVER

AMAZON RIVER,

BRAZIL

<u>Brazilian Paddlers</u>

They're here up a creek,
Their boat has a leak,
Their style is antique
But they paddle a streak.

We seek and critique
High tech as unique.
Still, the dugout can beat
A weak technique freak.

....and many an Amazon motor.

UCAYALI RIVER,

PERU

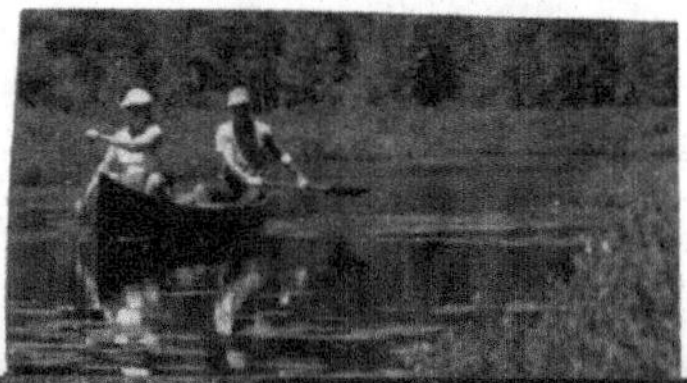

NORTH AMERICA – From Aboriginal to "Paddlesport"

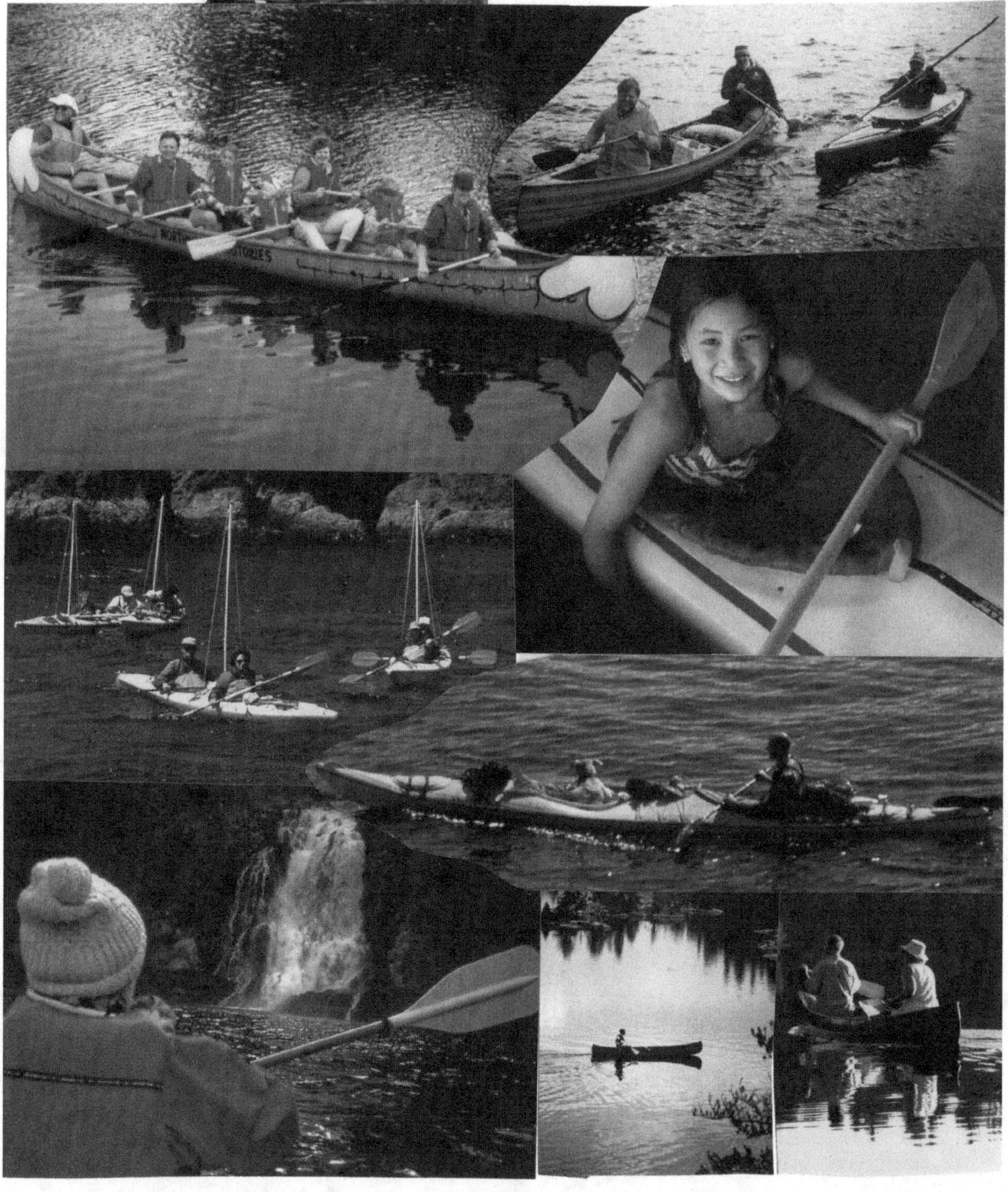

CANOES SCHMOOZE & KAYAKETY–YAK

"Tin Can" Meets "Furniture"

Days and miles from the nearest road.
Both are tough, and fun.
Safely rivers run.
......Just try not to broach with a load.

Wondrous whatchamacallit

(A Boat By Any Other Name...)

This craft is like a BOAT....
Born of the sea, designed by a salt.
Formed of wood, its bow flares wide,
Rising easily over large rolling waves.

Yeah, but it's also like a CANOE.....
You should call it a *"boanoe"*.

It **is** like a canoe....portageable
Thirteen feet long, thirty pounds light.
Built in the heartland by
A most artful creator of canoes.
Its stern is as sharp as the bow of a boat.

O.K., so let's say you've got a *"canoat"*.

Except that it's also like a KAYAK....
Requiring your bottom as ballast,
And a double paddle for balance and power.
Deck and skirt it goes without.
On an Eskimo roll you'd fall right out.

O.K., so it's a *"canoatyak"*?

I guess. Anyway it's good for kayakety~yak.
But its real name is....BEYOND.

Yes, it's a Canyak ——
No, a Kayoe ——
Or maybe a Kaycan,
Noeyak, or Yaknoe.
Don't matter none
What one calls this "canoe",
So long as she's fun
And "can—do" under you.

Reviewing the Fleet

There's the fifteen footer, for sunset schmoozin',
The North Bay Ugo is great for musin',
The Trout Creek and Sundance, for tripping and cruisin',
And Moores' bobbin' Buttercup is just plain amusin'.

The Mad River Monarch was a birthday gift,
The second Monarch gave us both a lift.
The double Klepper for togetherness,
The Feathercraft single when it's best with one less.

So which one is the best canoe?
"Would he have so many if he really knew?"

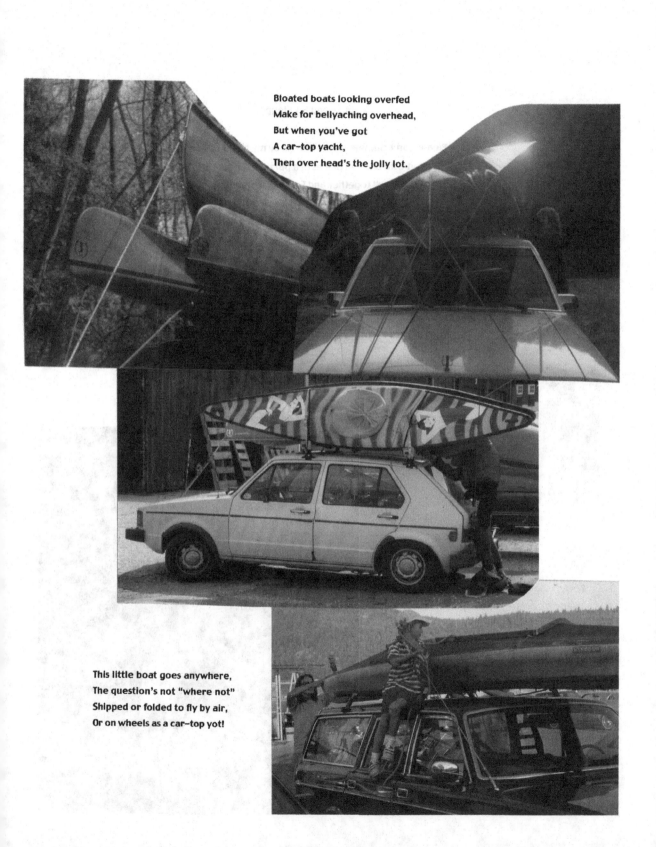

Bloated boats looking overfed
Make for bellyaching overhead,
But when you've got
A car-top yacht,
Then over head's the jolly lot.

This little boat goes anywhere,
The question's not "where not"
Shipped or folded to fly by air,
Or on wheels as a car-top yot!

A Skipper and His Klepper

Please don't stumble on the bundle by my bed.

It's filled with bits and pieces of a puzzle to be spread,

Then fit them all together and Eureka!, it's a boat,

The same that crossed from Europe and arrived here still afloat.

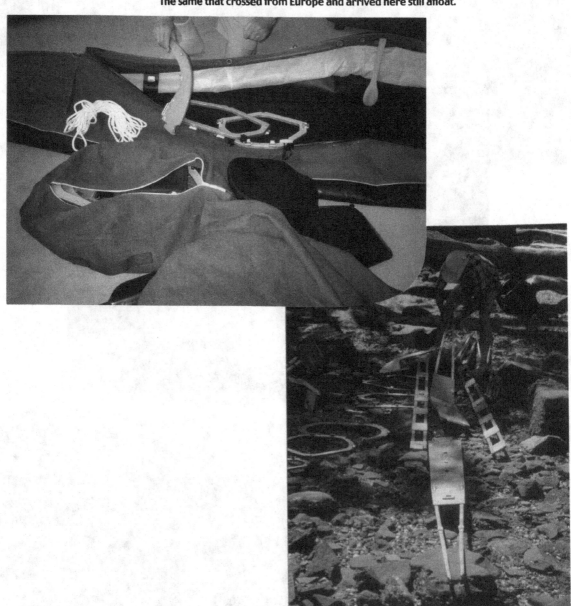

Thousands of miles
We've traveled together
My trusty kayak and I
    Through monstrous waves
    Of traffic we ply.

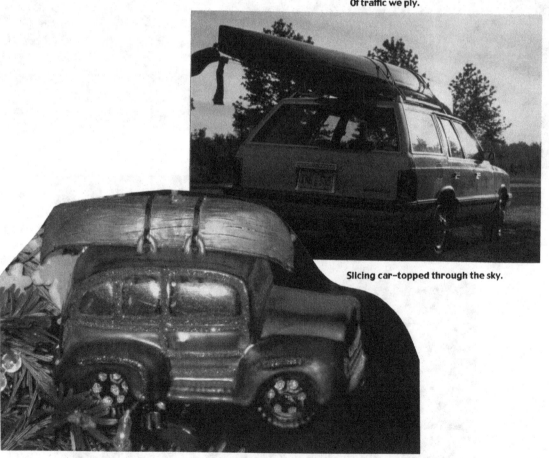

Slicing car–topped through the sky.

OCEAN RIVER PADDLING CLUB

Buy a wooden canoe ---
Not one found in the marts ---
And become a floating
Patron of the arts.

The Vanishing Varnished Canoe

Here's the unvarnished truth
On the varnished canoe.....

With the vanishing varnish
Went the times that we knew.

Find a River

Find a river
That you really like.
Then hope when you get there
It's not a turnpike.

The Poor Boat's Man

Who started this all,
Why do we still call
A canoe
The "poor man's yacht"?

I'm afraid it implies
The paddler's not wise,
Only poor.....
This is all that he's got.

Speed boats are like cars,
Some boats are just bars –
Prestigious pleasure lounges.

Then there are those who dote
On their skyscraper boat
Where you might hardly know
That you're afloat.

You focus on dials,
Sonic and scope.....
Sailing more by electronics
Than knowledge and hope.

Another way
To know the sea
Is close to water
Where I like to be.

Fundamentals and basics,
Tides and breezes we bear
Feeling the waves....
Smelling the air.

Paddling Your Own Canoe

When you dub the canoe "the poor man's yacht"
Does jogging become "the poor man's trot"?
I enjoy watching sports, theater too,
Can admire yachts, but choose to canoe.

It's a matter of style,
Not money, please note;
The real poor man's yacht
Is the parlor afloat.

A hundred-plus feet
At the waterline
Is what I own, yup,
It's all mine.

Those hundred-plus feet
Is why I got
A complimentary subscription
From <u>The Yacht.</u>

One hundred-plus feet
At the waterline,
Nautically sublime....
Grace afloat....

That is, should we ever
Line up our canoes
Plus add on the
Little boat.

Small

When you've downsized that cruise ship
To a cruising canoe...
Meals may be less sumptuous
But wow, what a view.

That go-anywhere sea-
Worthy kayak you've got
Is a gem of a "Small-
Is-Perfection" yacht.

Small is agile, mobile, simple,
Stretching money, time and space,
Saving energy, resources,
Your back; the human race.

ITEM: The Small Boat Shop in Norwalk, CT, has been taking in cruisers from skippers trading up to kayaks.

That cruiser (whose wash
Adds aliveness, by gosh),
With its engines growlin'
Three miles to the gallon,
Is its skipper, by G,
Having more fun than me?

'Stead of spending my wealth
I'm improving my health,
'Stead of paying insurance
I'm building endurance.
No lockage, no dockage, no agents a-callin'
I take no mauling on an annual hauling.

Well, he's having fun,
And so am I.
While he's sipping his rum
I drink wind, spray and sky.
I could imbibe later,
But I'm already high.

I peddle in the Springtime,
I paddle in the Summer.
While legs, then arms get toned real fine,
My middle stays a bummer.

From outside our kitchen window,

To across from Glacier Bay,

One happily flails;
One paddles with whales;
Now how are you
Spending YOUR day?

"Your arms are getting stronger."

"No, they're not.
Just longer."

Paddling long,
Sweating hard;
Just like galley slaves.

It's the
Monday–Friday tie
That binds;

Not fresh,
Free, weekend waves.

Build a House and Get to Paddle
......or just paddle.

I can't agree more, dear,
"Paddling's precious!"
You say.

Why this priceless canoe
Rents for almost three times our rental car
Per day.

Tickets Please

Cup your ears....close your eyes!
Paddling's been merchantized.
Victim to Disney commercialization,
Homogenization....Desensualization!

On the other hand
....Tomorrow's canoeists?

Choices

We don't dive waterfalls,
Claim no first descents,
Nor circumnavigate
Any continents.

We don't hype the high-tech,
We don't sell canoes.
We own no paddling rocket,
But can drift away the blues.

I don't beat out others,
For sport or otherwise,
Prefer to paddle curiously,
With the kids, my wife, the guys.

A little white water
And lots of lakes,
Memories of campsites,
High times, gentle wakes.

Our focus spreads beyond our time,
And is kind into the years.
For us here's the essence of space and joy,
Leaving little time for tears.

The "Lazy K" Stroke

Do we have to paddle
Incompatible?
Must kayaking double
Spell double trouble?

You chop up and down....
I try to pull sideways.
You splash a quick backhand....
I slowly slide wide ways.

We sit here creating
Our own stormy weather
On whether to feather
As we're tethered together.

Well, we forge a solution
From our on-board clinic.
Launch a great new style
(And a pacified cynic.)....

TEN STROKES YOUR WAY
Then, TEN STROKES MINE.
Each harbors his own
....Resting half of the time!

DO CANOES

AFTER A CRUISE

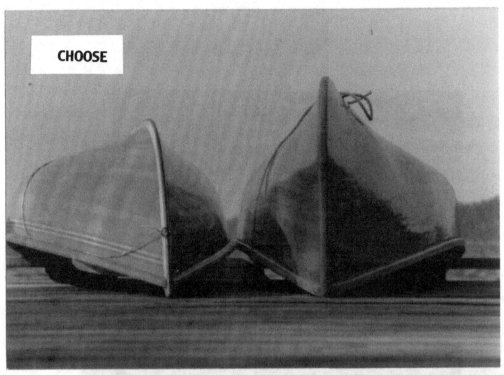

CHOOSE

TO SCHMOOZE ?

A Wooden Canoe Heritage Association's

CANOES SCHMOOZE

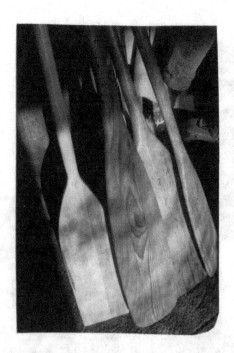

Spare Not the Paddle

The PADDLE? Fortuitous body extension,
Leveraging, powering,
Multiplying possibilities....
Accessing the inaccessible,
Paddle travel.

PADDLING, like walking,
Flows with unconscious ease.
Eyes scoping, all else automatically responds,
Body and craft as one.

The PADDLE may hasten our various escapes,
But more blissfully,
It's the artful key to undiscovered places.....
And truths.

PADDLING, the perfect blending
Of mind, body, spirit.
As I write my bones are begging:
"C'mon, let's GO!"

You could say that paddling is
A moving experience.
As for the paddle,
You wouldn't want to be up a creek
Without one.

Multiple Use

My taste in paddles is traditional,
New styles become conditional.
"T" grips, "S" shafts, plastic touches...
Some of these make better crutches.

FREELOADERS FOREWARNED

FRIENDLY NEIGHBORHOOD BAR

CLIMATE CHANGE?

(Cleaned, dried, and ready to pack away)

CANOEBIAL BLISS

"New Day a' Dawning"....
"Follow Your Bliss"....
"Life need never
Be better than THIS!"

Grab your wife,

Give her a kiss.
Then paddle off....
CANOE–BIAL bliss.

Saturday's "soldiers"
On Sundays....don't miss
Scooping up empties...

CAN–oebial bliss?

Paddle edge nudges a discarded empty,
Till it rises, and rolls ever-so-gently
Towards you,
Down the outstretched paddle,
Draining in fits and starts it approaches....
Now, don't miss.....
CAN–oebial bliss!

Misty morning,
Juices flowing,
Sunlight warming
Crispy air.

Off and touring,
Spirits soaring,
Sunshine pouring,
Not a care.

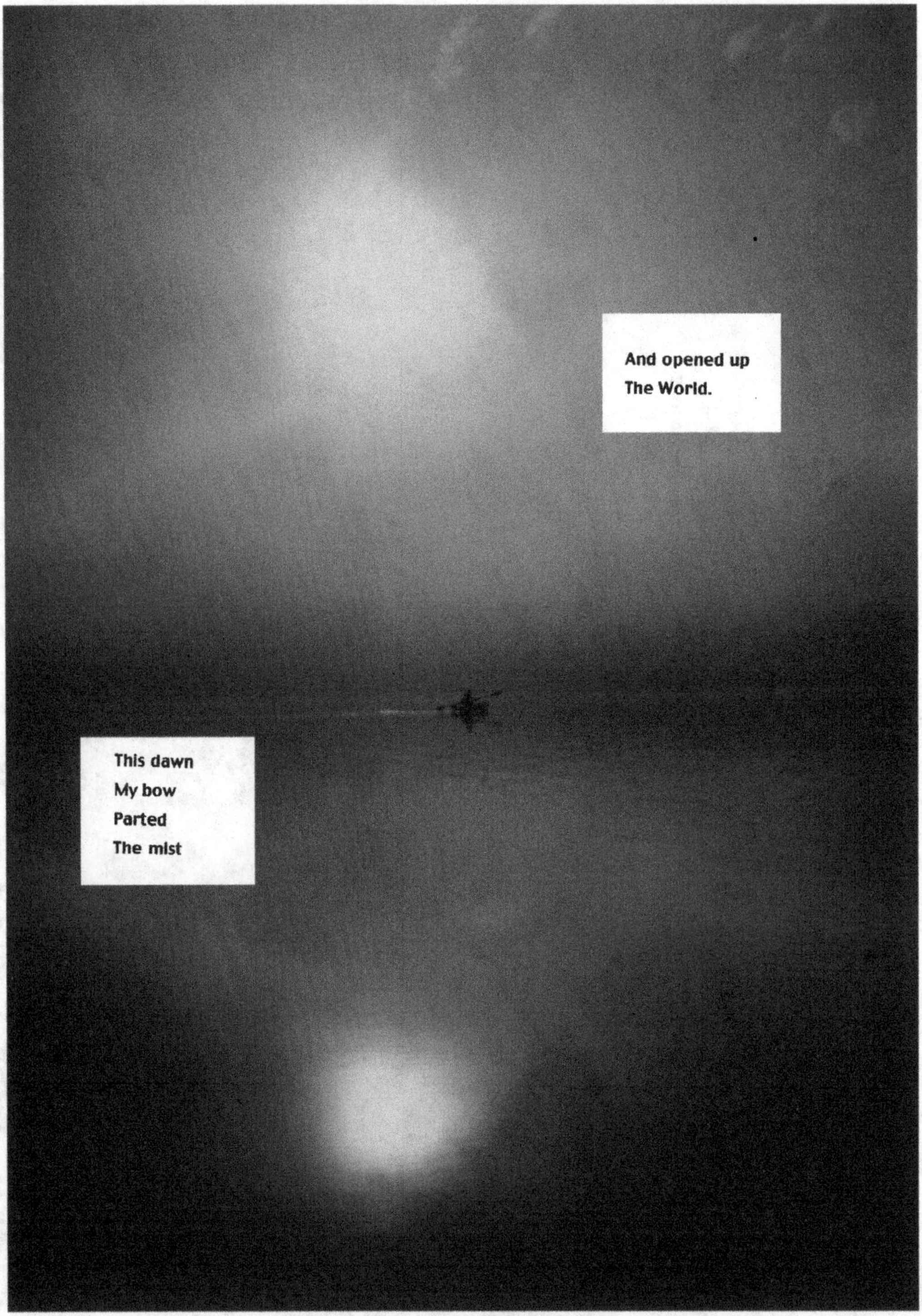

And opened up
The World.

This dawn
My bow
Parted
The mist

Alone

No paint—scraped rocks
No stumps of pine
No dams, no docks,
No tangled steel line
No bottles, no cans,
Fish still swim into view.
Oh to share this spot.....

But only with you.

Multi-Able

In country that's
Paddle-able, and
See-able,

Where I'm free-able
Be-able,
Me-able.

I guess that makes my kayak a
Multipurpose vehicle.

The Paddle as Joy Stick

Put in; stroke, drift....
>Languishing muscles welcome the invitation to stretch.
>A creaky unwinding; Little aches here and there
>Protest, and begin to vanish.
>Liberated eyes seek shoreline creatures
>Above, and skittering below.

Pull a bit, glide...
>Stiffness and kinks gone.
>Shifting gears into a gentle rhythm,
>Long thoughts, fresh insights,
>Soul soaking up stillness.

Thrust, fly...
>Cleansing breeze, purifying sun,
>Push–pull power. Off in overdrive.
>In "the zone"; light as air...
>Rising off the lake,
>Soaring with the clouds.

Collectibles

Some treasures sit in cases.

I sit in mine.

    Some investments ride out their lives in a vault.

    I ride in mine.

Most art is seen.

Mine is used.

    Some investments pay dividends that add to your wealth.

    Mine cures insomnia while building my health.

Most precious art is an object of beauty.

Mine also takes me to precious places of great beauty.

    Treasures are usually kept close to home.

    Mine gets me out and lets me roam.

Most art lends to quiet appreciation.

Mine also advances camaraderie, and spiritual reconstitution.

    Investments and treasures are subject to fashion and the state of markets.

    Mine are also subject to wind, and whim, the latter mostly mine.

My greatest treasure

Is the outdoor pleasure

That flows from my

"Collectible" canoe.

COLLECTIBLES II

This summer we collected islands.
One with seals, another with Indian graves. Islands to lunch on.
　　Islands to stretch on, to empty myself, to nap.

Islands with lichens, tidal pools, succulents, wild onion, raspberries,
　　bLackberries, neglected cabins, abandoned orchards, abandoned
　　dreams.
Islands with shell beaches, fishing shelters, scurrying mink, playful otter,
　　diving osprey, beach combing bear, blubberous seal lion, snag–sitting
　　eagle.

Pieces of shipwreck.
Weathered totem poles.
Pushing off, each a small world with its own story.

Eureka

I was a mobile global
In search of broader view.
I found it, true and noble
When, darling, I met you,,,

For years I'd roamed the world
Seeking that which might renew.
I knew my quest was ended
When I fell in love with
Your canoe.

The Kayakers

With non-elapsible car cum schlepper,
Its cargo collapsible gear, tent and Klepper,
To gem coves and beaches, the haven of choosers,
Far from land cruisers and wake-making bruisers.

Swimming with seals, strolling with seagulls,
Paddling with orca, gliding with eagles,
Not sittin' and sippin' in a RV park,
But butterfly-flittin' in a lighthearted lark.

From wheels to paddles, mile for mile
They've reached their paradise, all the while
Touching earth as a matter of style.....
"Traveling light, and with a smile."

.....Or maybe more a Cheshire grin?
(When seen again at Big Bucks Inn).
Adventures so pecunious
Make luxuries less ruinous.

Growing Sport

See the Japanese on vacation.
See them "doing" (snap)
Canoeing (snap snap)

They are not yet skilled, trained, disciplined,
Coordinated, organized, orderly
Or properly perfectionist, as they
Happily paddle about in their rented canoe.

They're having great fun,
And they're game to try.

Then, next year, they'll have something new
For you and me to buy.

Liquidate

Sell I.B.M.
For I bein'.

Sell your Pepsi
For think–young esprit.

Switch the Brothers Lever
For joie de vivre.

Sell General Motors
For north woods odors.

Trade your Frito–Lay
For more time to play.

Dump your U.G.I.
Tell them all goodbye.

Then buy a canoe
You to renew.

Which?

Does your eye rest on the condos...
    Or the cottage?
Do you see a shiny yacht...
    Or the canoe?

Here's ritzy and glitzy
    For the classy "you"
Then there's breezy and easy
    Like a friendly old shoe.

Lake Maligne

Paddling into a poster.
No sound track.
No commentary.
No people.

Background music?
Whatever's in your head....
Lapping waves the rhythm section.
Waterfall for a rising crescendo.
Distant thunder in the mountains.
A fast tempo finale.

I don't want a cabin cruiser,
Catered, or with crew.
Just give me northern time and space
With you in our canoe.

In a dull pewter sky
Dawn bursts golden and glows,
Warming my hands
And my heart.

SOLE PADDLERS
ARE
SOUL PADDLERS

NUTS & HEROES

Canoe Nuts

With happy wet thoughts,
Hearing sweet siren calls,
Canoe nuts hang boats
From the ceiling
And walls.

Romping!

Thrills!

Swamping......

Chills.

Like my canoe?
Call it a "nacht";
It's certainly not
Your typical yacht.

Like my canoe?
Call it a "not".
It's certainly nacht
Your typical yot.

I used to row a boat,
Now I'm a paddle gypsy.
It's less time in the oar house,
And more being close to tipsy.

<u>Deliverance</u>

She sees herself as a canoe widow,
Sees me out there breasting the waves,
Riding the Red Lady for all she's worth
With the other canoe nut knaves.

But, most noble mission of mercy
(Which I hesitate to tout)
Concerns comfort and security
In behalf of the "house of out".

I'd rather have
A canoe fetish
Than
A shoe fetish.

Kneelin',

If not appealin'
Has a revealin' facet ---
The ballast asset.

Certified Pioneer

It was well after the season,
Lake returning to reason.
Crisscrossing cruisers gone, nothing to do.

Shore reflections quite still,
Pastel mists, blazing hill,
Lazily sculling beneath cloudless blue.

In an Indian sweater,
Battered hat, giant feather,
And plaid shirt in an October hue.

Suddenly, unpleasant fate,
My peace and quiet evaporate
As alien sounds and frowns charge into view.

Angry pistons roaring down,
Bearing kids with unearned power.
Summer throwback, circling round,
Not discouraged by my glower.

Macho play at something new...
Not yet paddling their own canoe,
Taunting, "Hey, a pioneer!"
Now there's a cause for cheer...
Maybe someday they'll play pioneer too.

The Making of Men

Why do "traditional" canoe camps choose
To deliberate;y use heavy wood–canvas canoes
That actually soak up water additionally
To twenty and thirty pounds...quite intentionally?

Now add solid wood wannigans, portage dreading,
Large fire irons and axes add to the sweating,
And thick cotton tents...forget any netting.
Why? It's old–fashioned manhood we're forging, abetting.

If the well–to–do young are bored
Because they've never worked,
Get them out on a trip
Where the "work" can't be shirked,

And it works.

These "do or die" awful moments become,
With Mother Nature's help,
Coming–through success stories,
Growth spurt, standing tall,
Fond memories, lifetime friendships,
Proud Dad...
Worth the money.

A family canoe outing lets a parent realize the growth potential and strength of their offspring. Send the kid to camp, then let him or her take you out.)

Teamwork

Lenore and Jane went kayaking.

Dropped off at the edge of the Pacific by the MV "Lady rose",
And officially briefed on the crowded bobbing float,
Lenore startled the ranger:
      "Can we come over to your island if it rains?"
Jane just blushed, the others paddled off,
New adventures unfolding.
But Lenore's requests grew:
      "Can we see your place?"
      "Got any coffee? Tea's O.K."
      "Can we ride in your boat?"
      "Join you on your rounds?"
      "How about dinner at your cabin?"
      "Can we have salmon?"
And days later of the returning "Lady Rose":
      "Can we stay on?"
Of the ship-to-shore, the agents, the bookings' list, the sailing schedule:
      "Five days? Three?"
Of the bridge, the mate, the beleaguered skipper:
      "Aw, please! we've missed out!"
Of the passengers crowding the rail:
      "C'mon everybody, all in favor yell aye!"
      "Til tomorrow? That's GREAT! Yippee!"

With vocal Lenore out for more and more
Quiet Jane remained almost a stranger.
Roaring Lenore got all she asked for.
And Janie, she got the ranger.

Ukulele Canoodle

He had hitchhiked north four hundred miles
To be met by a roofless jalopy
And a girl full of smiles,
Fresh sweet eagerness, alluring and real...
The flowers in the dashboard vase,
And the girl behind the wheel.

Exams and winter gladly packed away,
Carefree reunion on a sultry spring day,
Last summer's romance, where would it now go,
Here on the river of Henry Thoreau?

From the past season's boys' camp, and hers of girls,
Separated by a mile of coast,
Joined after taps by stealth canoes,
Then severed...forever?...but for the post.

They remembered the beer tied and towed off the stern –
"Cool!" (and well out of sight).
And the scary view down from the macho cliff's leap –
"You don't HAVE to dive..so lead with your feet."

Now cruising Concord's winding stream,
They canoodled, expressing no cares,
Until under the sacred North Bridge,
Sensing history...the nation's...theirs....

He earnestly resumed his strumming,
She barely repressing a smile,
He worked at being a caricature,
And she knew exactly why...

Moving onward, the river, she, he,
They parted in a glen,
Having created a final sweet memory,
Knowing they'd meet not again.

Jump For Joy

Sandy Campbell, topnotch surgeon, conservationist,
Builder of log cabins and railroads,
Has been a canoeist since age seven; never stopped.

He would paddle next to a swimming moose,
Jump onto its back
And ride it almost to shore.

To this his bride can testify,
And this I urge you not to try.

Sure solid grip...
Handle on the world.

Dragon Boats

Spirit powers their boats.
Together with humor and heart,
They dare and ride their dragon ---
"Dragons Abreast", "Abreast in a Boat",
"Bosom Buddies", "Warriors of Hope".

Their dragon is cancer.

Royal Simplicity

Ted Moores
Lived with his love,
Squeezed into a tiny Algonquin log cabin
In order to pursue his other passion,
Building perfect canoes.
Each took all of his being.

One day he was shocked to find
The underside of a Rolls Royce dashboard
Unfinished.
Every part of a Moores canoe,
Even the hidden places,
Are lovingly complete.

We picked up our Butternut, glowing.
Then marveled at, sitting under a tree,
Varnished, inlaid,
His last canoe off the mountain.
"Too beautiful to paddle," I said.
"Tougher than those plastic discount boats," he replied.

Two weeks later we saw that canoe on T.V.,
On the Scottish honeymoon, paddled by Charles and Diana,
A wedding gift from Canada's paddling Prime Minister.
Born from the elegance of a one-room Ontario cabin,
A reflection of pride and perfection.

This man preserved a heritage,
Active, healthy, free;
While sports went commercial,
Sagging couches and paunches
We cheer and drink beer with T.V.

Canadians are also ball–batty,
But to a lesser degree;
They call Bill Mason
Their own "Babe Ruth"
Which makes them heroes to me.

Paddlers......Resting

CANOE VIEWS

CLOSE TO THE WATER

Earth's nurturing
Free flow,
A paddler's view.
Fleeting
Reflections:
The prism is you.

Dips and curls,
Drips of pearls,
Ripples and swirls,
Meld my worlds.

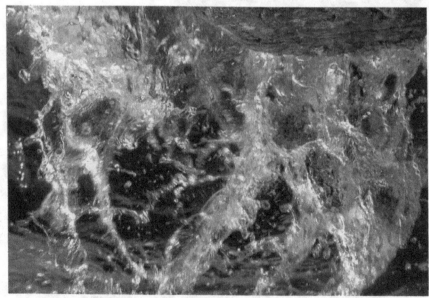

The lake was
Like glass,
'Til you wiggled
Your ass.

Scout this hyper-spastic free flow.
Check out its temperature.
To be a sun-warmed voyeur, or
Hypothermic voyageur.

"Right down the 'V'!"
   "Let's wait and see..."
"DIG it! The 'V'!!"
      "Eeeeeee

         eeeee

            eee...."

Living worlds
Where paddles go;

Of sparkling sun
And H2O.

Two worlds, one world?
Above. Below.

All nature's one
....Wet paddlers know!

Touch a billion years ago,
Glittering veins of quartz,
Voyageurs from a molten interior.
Born well before the creation
Of eyes that love their spidery insistence,
Or minds that picture geologic surges,
Prehistoric....
Post–historic.

Insistent roots filling
Lifeless cracks....
Odd?
Or the true face of God?

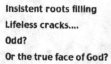

Left traffic lights
For star–bright nights
And a sun–burst dawn
Flashing "GO", paddle on.

Gliding suspended
Between bottom and sky,
Mist lifting, sun rising
To a natural high.

In the Mainstream

Fragile fading leaf
Spinning, floating down
Trying to keep up
Trying not to get hung up
Tiny curled-up leaf
Tumble-swirling through...
I am you.

Winking paddle
Stirring sunlight
Crystal bright
Nirvana Lite.

GUNKHOLING

From a downsoft morning,
Drifting quiet and loose...
Raucous squawks
From Mother Goose.

Christmas in August

Finally, morning;
Rushing madly,
Down to my toys
Sitting under the tree,

I put one in
And paddle off ---
Borne again,
I'm free!

September Song

Reading today's article on nursing homes
Sent me dashing out to do
My neglected regular paddle.

Added minutes, a few new aches.
But this was less marathon,
More floating through picture postcards.

Here and there frosted leaves stood out,
Hanging still on empty branches
While most had blown away with autumn's blast.

I'm for clinging like those that last.

Stocking Up for Winter

The lake of my dreams has
        Clear deep waters under lichen–covered cliffs,
        Reflecting tall pines, birches and sunny blue–berried knolls,
        Its breezes carrying
        The perfume of sweet fern and balsam.

The lake of my dreams has
        Thousands of tiny minnows among the newly sunken spruce,
        Big fellows cruising just beyond,
        An elder fish exposing himself along the shore.

        It has a family of loons that swim over to greet one,
        Martens jumping from rock to rock,
        Squeaking kits in a beaver house,
        Otters that dash up to play,
        Brassy bass that curiously follow my paddle strokes,
            A black bear who licks out my beached canoe.

The lake of my dreams has
        Ancient campsites, flat rocky points for cooking up a catch,
        Inviting islands with high nestled niches
        From which one can stare down into mysterious depths
        Or lie back, cushioned, to gaze at a sky full of featherbed clouds.

The lake of my dreams is....
        REAL.

Every summer I portage to it, and paddle
In solitary ecstasy,
Winter's nourishing memories confirmed.
I tank up on the whole enriched mixture
For another year's journey,
The circle back to here!

<u>Head Laundry</u>

Paddle strokes start my songs,
Speak to my soul,
Gently clean, rinse, sort and stack
Assorted laundry of the mind
To, as ads tell us,
Something lighter, and brighter.

Paddling also lets my body hang loose, stretch and air,
Which makes it ever righter, and me less up–tighter.

Out there, where the lakes and trees are
My head laundry dries where it's breezier.

Where others seek peaks, or a monastery,
My paddle pursues a new tributary.

Hear the Laughing Wind

There's a promise as we venture forth
Combatting wind and waves,
Those very forces overcome....
Should make the run home fun.

Then why so often when we're out
Relishing return with ease,
Those winds reverse and make perverse
Our plan to sail the breeze.

Condensation Weather Report

When morning's fresh dew
Clings to your canoe
This weatherwatch forecasts
The sky will be blue.

Tea and Tenacity

He saw the weather unsettled, but wanted to paddle.
She used a dreary morning to join a neighbor for lunch.

He launched and paddled off, making use of lee shores.
Approaching a bay, he stretched with the wind, quartering the waves.
She had tea.

Gusts grew in velocity,
Half way across a full squall, roaring like a freight train.
No onward progress, the challenge now to stay upright.
She was enjoying her visit, and a second cup of tea.

He, managing to turn on a wave, surfed into a cove,
Out of wind's way, riding the swells.
Recovering, he carefully picked his way home,
Arriving with the first cheerful burst of sun.

"How was your lunch?"
"Nice. How was your paddle?"
"Nice."

I travel in water,
It travels in me.
Primal life source revealed
When I have to pee.

Whether Report

Silver slivers breaking through
Scudding puffs of gray,
Sunshine's streaks of glory signal
Hope this soulful day.

Sudden gustings,
Waves rising,
Wind's frightening roar.

So glad to be
Watching all this
From the shore.

Precon–See'd

That shiny "tin can"?
Just a water–splashed rock;
"Broken glass"....fiery drops of dew.
The "tower"'s just trees
Standing strong in the breeze,
"Tossed paper"?...white birch, in close view.

That adrift "plastic bag"....
Just the feather of a gull.
More "glass"?...beads of quartz rocks besmirch.
The "dock"'s just a giant
Bleached log, hard, defiant.
"Plastic cup?" You guessed it, more birch.

　　　We come to the woods
　　　Careful not to despoil
　　　But bring baggage that litters the mind.
　　　Let wildness reveal
　　　The real from the "real",
　　　Better not just to "see", but to find.

Natural foam

Foam with white quartz

Frothy Math/Humping Home

For starters, when is 2 the difference between 5 and 1?
And when is knowledge *less* power?
When not having to power against the tide.

Tide flowing 2 knots ....happy assistance.
U–turn, return, becomes 2 knots resistance.
2 knots to my 3 = 5 knots....yippee!
But my 3 knots, minus 2,
Becomes 1...don't you see?

Tide, the friend that can turn on you.
Just as bad when you do the turning.
From gurgling helpful frothy foam
To pushing, plowing, humping home.

<u>**Love Will Out**</u>

Spring brings the huge snapper
To the surface,
Prowling, bumping my canoe.

On the distant shore
Another, even larger armor-plated, iron-jawed
Scowling chomper cruises listlessly.

Oh, to be a matchmaker here,
Producing....
The world's biggest snapping turtles.

He reads my mind.
I read his eyes;
"NO......MORE.......BLIND DATES!"

****

Two weeks later I witnessed what appeared to be a newly
underwater erupting volcano. Without any help from me
these great uglies had found one another. All that remains
to be said is, swim here?

Multiplicity of Curiosities

Bursting forth from the deep,
Orca surround us,
Curious, friendly, playful,
A few mock charges.

Suddenly from the north
A floating skyscraper appears, halts,
Loudspeakers proclaiming,
Its decks and lounges a gallery of shoulder to shoulder spectators.
This multiplicity of curiosities
Becomes a three-ring eco-tour show,
Occasioned by a pod of curious celebrity orca.

Kayakers
Playing among the islands,
Watching by-passing
Cruise ships
Which mostly play
With themselves.

Off-Trail Lake

Out there,

Between the world as we know it, and heaven,

Lies a lake which is still as it once was,

With me as I like to be.

On that lake I feel oneness and onlyness,

With welcome interruptions: the once-shy loon couple

Now swims over to display their young.

Yesterday three otters dashed

To play with my cast and cavort at my feet.

Every new vista triggers a memory:

The children discovering stars....

Friends thrilling to their first fish....

A couple rediscovering each other....

The old prospector's camp....

Where we skinny–dipped....

Where I opened my retirement champagne on the day after Labor Day....

And let the day's catch swim off, sharing my freedom.

It's fun to pursue the clues
To age-old processes,
And to unravel a mystery or two
Among the many in this
Gigantic embracing wilderness.
A tree falls in the forest, and because I am here
It is heard, and this summer part of a cliff
Of rock, two billion years old, crumbled into the lake
Honoring my presence without making me a participant.

One can spot the aboriginal sites....
The flat easy-to-camp spots
Served by prevailing breezes.
Just by adopting their natural lifestyle,
One finds the most comfortable niches,
And they seem worn above the best fish holes.
An encyclopedic detail of fishing lore emerges
From my perch high on an island cliff,
And by gliding slowly along its aquarian shores.

Like the flit of a paddle flash,
The whole day passes in an instant.
The portage back , through fragrant forest,
Is further inebriated with fresh thoughts and new convictions.
A magic time in a fantasy place
More real than most of what I'm heading back to.

This is my lake,
But only in that I've gotten
To know it better than anyone else.

Even better than select pristine corners like this,
Lying between earth and heaven
Would be their more abundant existence,
Vital preserves
Safely part of our daily world....
And closer to home.

Urban Paddlers

Kayakers and canoeists are rediscovering their local working harbors. For many it's the closest water. Rental and instructional facilities are sprouting accordingly.

Victoria, on Vancouver Island, is a high-traffic harbour , but nonetheless welcoming. Paddlers here, as increasingly elsewhere, can enjoy a civilized mix of the natural and the industrial. (Note: Canadians have "u" in their harbours.)

Launch from downtown's Pebble Beach, and paddle left;
Passing whale watchers and float planes
To the ivied Empress Hotel, with its hanging baskets,
And a giant floral bed before Parliament stretching its message:
W.....E....L....C....O....M....E

Continue up the Gorge
Between the bustling shipyard
And the mighty jaws of the car crusher,
A working harbour of kaleidoscopic busyness
Transforms to...a reversing falls.

Or put in and paddle to the right;
Where snow-covered Olympics backdrop
Barnacled islands festooned with purple and orange starfish,
Geese nesting, otters cavorting, and
Curious seals circling you with their young.

Between the inland falls and outer islands lies all of Victoria...
This Queen city of salt and nectar,
Of First Nations and all nations,
Where honest sweat mingles with active leisure
And funky meets elegance.
Here plenty of harbour,
And smiles to go around.

Scurrying ferries and the roar of the airborne,
Small cruise ships and large sand barges,
Fishing boats and yachts,
Racing canoes and rowing shells,
Swinging construction cranes,
Planes diving down through the "keyhole",
Resonant arrivals on the fore deck of the "Coho",
A bustling working harbour,
And everywhere, flowers.

But all is not roses.
Fishing boats carry their own smell of the sea.
Float planes do roar.
The scrap yard clangs and grumbles as it crunches cars.
The last incoming "Coho" blankets town with its deep throated whistle at 11:30 PM, sleepy time.
The crew coaches yell and growl across still waters at 6 AM – forget more sleepy time...
But their crews win Olympic medals.
There are outlet pipes...and volunteers who monitor them.
There is flotsam and jetsam...and a boatman who clears and removes.
There are buoy and speed violators...and a patrol boat that sets things straight, very nicely, in fact, to
new arrivals.

It's everyone's harbour,
Circled not by fences and forbidding signs,
But a harbour ringing walkway,
Not just for meandering tourists,
But morning backpacks, briefcases, strollers,
And evening grocery bags heading home,
Commuter cyclists...and kayakers,
Joggers....powered wheelchairs.
An elderly couple in a canoe,
A tea party under the totem poles.
Lovers, and grandchildren.

Paddle in the evening, glide like the seagulls
Who bank towards a seal
And come up with herring.
A mink starts down the sidewalk,
Steps aside for a crab–carrying gull.
Otters roll around off the rocks,
Sometimes with a spectacular water ballet of lovemaking.
And an eagle flies off, in his talons – a gull.

Dusk...the heron,
Silhouetted against city lights
Reflected in the watery mirror at end of day stillness.
Smell of salt, seaweed...and always the flowers.

Victoria, a working harbour...that welcomes canoes and kayaks,
Working pretty well.

Saturday

I'd rather be out a sea'n
Than saw'n all this wood.
I'd rather see a chop at sea
Than me a-choppin' wood.

I'd rather aim for distant shores
Than guide the chain saw home.
Instead of hauling boat, then logs
I'd really rather roam.

I'd rather be out splitting waves
Before the autumn fog.
I'd rather log a day at sea
Than spilt another log.

Chopping warms us twice, Frost said,
For me it comes to three.
A slow burn brings this note to head;
I've run away to sea.

Plugging In to Nature's Internet

When you're cruising in your canoe,
Do you hear lapping voices?

Whimsical whispers on things you might do?
Brainstorming bolts from out of the blue?
Fanciful flashes that seem to shine true?
Insightful slices that bow–cut right through?
Outrageous assumptions, in a purple–pink hue?
Outlandish presumptions, but sparkling new?

You do?
Me too!

But I only catch the muse
When I'm messing in canoes;
Sort of putting in and paddling out
To catch up on the news.

The Lake to All Places

This lake, stroke,
Leads, stroke,
To all places.

This boat, stroke,
Floats, stroke,
Through a sea
Of memories and faces.

In the fog beyond
Lies someday;
Meanwhile, how great to be out here
On a Monday.

WHITEWATER

We think of whitewater in terms of thrills, and skills.

Lots of big water, ignored until recently, has become popular with rafting and play boats. Thrills, and not without the skills.

For backcountry tripping, those whitewater skills can become essential to comfort if not survival. They include knowing when to scout, line, run, run empty and when to portage. Skills, not without thrills.

Local rivers and outfitters are a great way to experience whitewater basics and to develop skills.....with perhaps many a Saturday or weekend return....because of the thrills.

Inherit the Flow

"Just flow with the river".....
Darn good advice
For success with white water,
And the river of life.

Steer, don't resist
When it comes to obstruction.
Let the river insist,
But you point direction.

Back paddle when needed,
Draw, pry, and brace.
Harnesss the onward.
The river sets the pace.

Zen Interrupted

Dumping; thorough dunking;
Splashing soul awake.
Flashing icy-dicey insight
That trumps my meditative state.
Springing loose insistent truths
That urgently relate.....
For now, forget Nirvana,
Rehabilitate.

Cool. Very!

Whitewater, smashing!
      Hey, stop splashing.
Look. We're turning.....
      Please stop churning.
Good. we're making it......
      You mean scraping it.
Yo! We're bumping......
      It's called dumping!
Cool!
      Fool!

Some pass through.....
Others dumps and soaks....
Different strokes
For different folks.

Advice from the Stern

When we blow our own horn
We're a little less likely
To ride a churning river....
Uprightly.

Those who split their attention
Between paddle and horn
Are a little more likely
To be white water shorn.

No matter that players
Might like to toot.
There are forces in rivers that
Don't give a hoot.

White Water Choice

I don't like the "alum"
For it's constant
"Boom, boom."
But it's better in fact
Than a single "ca–RACK!"

Paddle Your OWN Canoe?

"Paddle your own canoe"
If it's cruising you do.
But when whitewater bent,
I'd rather rent.

RX –iver

Paddle allergic,
Terrible itch,
Rising blood pressure
To double stroke pitch;

Prognosis? Solution?
Something properly rash...
Feverish highs call for
A whitewater bash.

PADDLING WITH KIDS

ME do it!

GETTING READY

READY!

She was half the size
Of her busy paddle,
With energy left
        For non-stop prattle.

Chatting and dipping
From the great wide bow seat
Until 2 P.M. nap-time
When she......fell asleep.

Icky, squishy,
Ookie, gookie,
Mooshy, smooshy
Fun.
But a nice clean sport?

<u>Naturally Kids</u>

Little Laurie would happily show off her "canoe muscle" to great big adults, who'd say things like:

"Aren't you afraid the bears will get you?"

"You'll never catch me sleeping on the ground."

"I'd miss my shows."

"I'd miss my showers."

"It sounds like work to me."

"No, we have fun."

"But what do you do all day?"

And the kids might say,

"Swim, fish, paddle, play games, make up games, songs, plays,

Go exploring, find stuff, pick berries, draw, read, make collections, build things,

Catch crayfish, feed chipmunks, listen to beaver kits inside their lodge..."

To which we might add:

Learn to cook, and love it

Work without considering it work, like managing waves, portages, making camp

Discover aborigine sites, hunting camps, old logging camps, trapper's cabins

Look up into a heaven filled with stars and mystery.

Kids take to the out-of-doors...naturally, like

Ducks to water....

Otters to slides....

Chipmunks to bannock

Loons to minnows....

Beavers to poplar....

Bass to worms

And, yes, gulls to fish guts....

Mosquitoes to Judy....

Whiskey Jacks to anything.

Resisting the "childhood moving indoors" trend,

Tapping into that school of knowledge

And skills run not by adults, but Mother Nature.

Daily engagement in the "real world",

Because, they'll tell you,

"It's Fun!"

Bow-girl,
Muscle.
"Wanna tussle?"

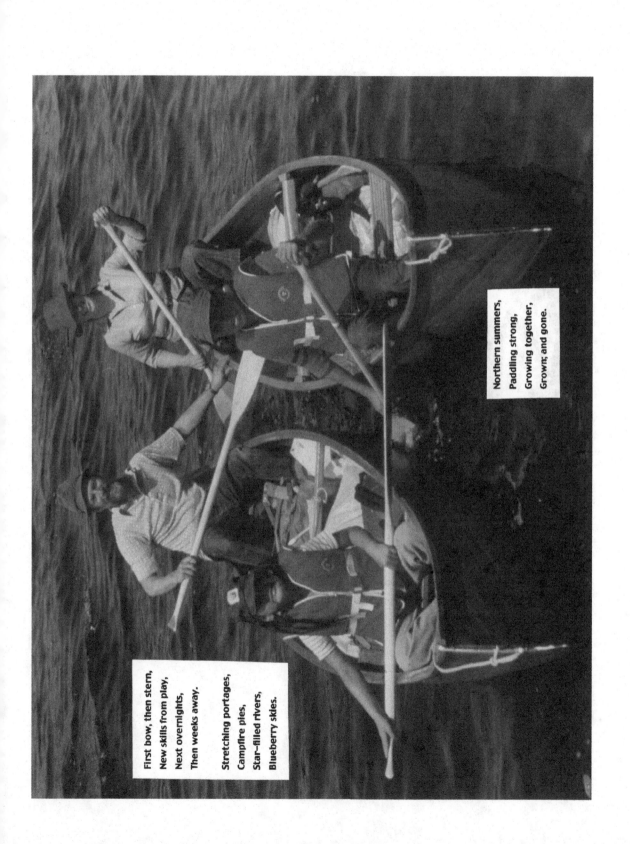

First bow, then stern,
New skills from play,
Next overnights,
Then weeks away.

Stretching portages,
Campfire pies,
Star–filled rivers,
Blueberry skies.

Northern summers,
Paddling strong,
Growing together,
Grown, and gone.

Don't throw stuff around and mess up a pretty place......

Or you know what?
The peenie–biting pike
Will GET you.

And you know what?
Mother Nature will be MAD!
And maybe Smoky Bear
Will GET you.

School's O.K.

.....but THIS IS O.K.er!

Someday, I swear,
It'll be my turn.
But they'll be in their rocking chairs
Before I get to stern.

When a picture is worth
A thousand swear words.

<u>**On Paddling with Two Wonderful But Nonetheless Teenage Girls**</u>

"That's what she said you said I said."
"No....That's what you said she said I said."
"Listen....I said what she said you said, but..."

I'm saggin' not from paddlin'
But the prattlin' up ahead.
Just pray I stay a draggin'
'Stead of a naggin' dragon head.

Conservation is
My prime concern
...So I never fight
For bow
....or stern.

Hey Kids, Remember This Character-Building Day?

Windbound shore,
Dawn of decision.
Go? Or no!

Gusts punctuated fitful sleep.

Measuring their fury and direction,
From crashing waves to.....
Shifting now? Lighter lappings?
New bursts. But diminishing?
Spill forth, or a soft uneasy roll back to half-sleep?

Our third day here,
Perhaps just imagining a lull,
Desire triumphs over weary helplessness...
It's "Foxfire!", or was your action code, "Firefox!"?

Tents collapse.
Each pre-packed bag swings into place.
Positioned canoes are afloat.
All tension channeled to getting off, and moving water.

Yesterday we were blown back.
Now, beyond the point, bows meet the wind,
Stagger, dip, roll....
Shore-bound muscles aching to perform...
We inch ahead.

By wind's full anger
We crossed to more protected shores,
Mile by grateful mile.
Almost home, and...
Then.... through the Narrows....
Wind! Full force!

Forty-five minutes to paddle just half a kilometer to the dock
In waves that often hid us from each other.
Home...in driving sleet – up an iced-over path

It was still August.

But here's the point:
That instant of decision was correct,
Not by circumstance, but by commitment.
You came through, kids.
This is why some parents send their children to camp.
And why some parents don't.

Graduation

He carried his canoe
First time....usually I portaged both.
On a mile and a half portage
He proudly brought his a mile.

Then each of us helped
The other finish.
We spoke of challenge, and cooperation.

At portage end, gamely smiling,
And drained....he was too tired to swim.
Supper revived, for a rollicking good time,
But very brief, before crashing to sleep.

Summer Spurt

Sunshine, chores,
Fertile space....
Broadening shoulders
To take my place.

Surprise!

The GOOD news is
> Your kids DO pick it all up.
> Learning, doing, going along.
> There comes a time when
> They'll want you to go with them
> Where once you guided and led.

The BAD news is
> Try keeping up.

Water, water, everywhere,
We need no kitchen sink;
Proper etiquette out here
Is what meets needs, I think.

We travel on water
And pee like we oughter
And sweat till we manage a rest.

We drink from the sky.
Does God ever cry?
Water from heaven tastes best.

CANOE DOG

CANOE DOG –
Our undisputed
Self-appointed
Significant other.

We love our dog Fritzi,
But she's awfully frisky.
Taking her out
Appeared to be risky.

We had to restrain her
Though it sometimes seemed cruel
'Til certified by
"Canoe Obedience School".

With selective hearing
Except for grandmother.

Cheese and crackers
Paddle snack....
"Snoopy" hopes we
Turn our back.

Okay!
I'll sit very still
('Til next time).

Nice crossing.

Maybe not....
But I'd go for it.

Lunch?!

Catch any?

Ooops!

Lie down,
Stay low,
No jump out 'til I say
"O.K.", or ""Go!"

    "O.K. kids,
    Let's GO."

    "Home, James."

TRIPPING & CRUISING

From Traces to Spaces

Traveling light and without much fuss
As gypsies we're amphibious,
Whenever we're able to freely roam
God's special places...and cheaper than home.

With folding shelter
And portable boat
We expand our scope
From new spaces afloat.

Far from ghettos of RV's
Tightly packed in the sun,
Camping with whales
Off a beach is more fun.

Totem poles and tidal pools,
Misty fiords and salmon streams,
Towering trees and snowy peaks,
Majesty beyond our dreams.

From Temagami to Tofino, we
Camp and paddle most joyfully
With joi de vivre and esprit
'Cause everything, plus us, is free.

"Roughing " It

Sun's last rays flirt with the horizon,
Its beams back lighting wildflowers;
Savory dinner, perfected over coals...
Silence...distant loon calls echoing...

Far from the urban dance
That crazily schemes, then sanctions
Each new encroachment.

Tired muscles our night cap.
Crisp wholesomeness our tonic.
Another northern night descends.

Deploring the Roaring

I awake to the crashing of
Surf on the shore:

Only to find it's
The roar of your snore.

Contrasts

When you've moved from citified service
To do-it-all yourself
And grown from cog, to captain,
To recognized woods elf,

It's the contrast that's so groovy,
Why else swizzle in the drizzle?
Complicity with simplicity –
And complexities can fizzle..

Tingling drops cool a tiring run;
Gentle warming when the shower is done,
Grey clouds shade after sweltering sun...
With surprises in the occasional one.

Welcoming north winds after a muggy day,
Thankful shelter in a protected bay.
A cold water dive cleanses sweaty skin;
Glad to be out after glad to be in.

Portaging the lot with your own strength and beef,
End of trail wonder, euphoric relief.
A flat cozy haven that's not windblown,
A soft niche to stretch every worn-weary bone

Singing to match rhythmic paddle strokes
Star-filled stillness, bawdy bedtime jokes.
A well-placed tarp against the rain,
And deep sleep easing unaccustomed strain.

Steaming coffee on a morning that's briskly cold,
Sweet berries, crisp bannock, flipped high and bold.
Evening's extravaganza that eventually
Fills that demanding spot that's been feeling empty.

The muscle-stretching walk after days of slack
During which, thank heavens, you've recovered your back.
The balm of lazy fishing after days so hectic
Until that strike so seismic and electric.

Contrasts lively tripping make
Like seasons on a northern lake.
Some from fervent prayers called,
Some arrive welcomed not at all.

Water resisting, craft responding,
Contrasts blending and opposites bonding.
New muscles relish the onward journey.
Nothing here for an attorney.

100 Unnamed Lakes No More

We first thrilled
In unnamed lakes
By naming them
After ourselves ---
        Judy Lake, Lake Judith, Lak Saint Judith
Now, like the Native Peoples,
We name them ---
And rename them ---
By their living significance.
        Blueberry Lake, Blueberry Pancakes Lake, Lots of Frogs Lake,
        Gourmet Dinner Lake.
There's also Blister Lake, Bee-Sting Lake, and Lake Ache.

We know a Hungry Lake, No Supper Lake, Bad Daddy Lake,
As well as a Lake Delicious Steak.

And Heron Lake, Polliwog Lake, Largest Garter Snake Lake,
Lake Clearbottom and Lake Bare Bottom.

Lots of Lost Lakes. Lost Lure Lake,
Lost Sneaker Lake,
Lost Dog Lake; and Found Dog Lake (or
Graduation From Senior Puppy to Junior Dog Lake).
There are no Lost Virtue Lakes in the family atlas.

Friendly Duck Lake, Lake Browse-Line, Lake Otterslide,
Lake Hungry Fish, Fish Used-To-Be-Here Lake,
No Fish --- None! Lake.

Longest Portage Lake, Hidden Lake, Oh, Sweet Lake.
Lake Macintosh's Toffee, Lake Peanut Butter Banquet,
Spruce Juice Lake, Lake Diarrhea.

Lake Late Arrival, Don't Bother with the Tarp – It Isn't Going to Rain
                Lake,
Lake New Leader.

Loon Association Meeting Lake, Fly-in Garbage Dump Lake

Boots of the Dutch Prince Lake, Someone Left Sneakers Exactly My Size
Lake,
Where Sandy Jumped Onto the Swimming Moose's Back Lake,
Lake Storm at Dinner, Last of the Rum Lake.

Lake Windbound, Lake Effluent,
Lake Aspirin, Lake Aspiration,
Lake Revelation (or The Birds-and-Bees Talk Lake).

Big Bear Lake, Big Mosquito Lake, Big Bird Lake,
Big Bard Lake, Lake Big Wind.

HEARD---

When all those mosquitoes are trying to get OUT of our tent ---

    "Sorry , I'll soap up."

When wind or current seem oddly strong, should the bow insist on a spell at stern?

    "Sorry, I was praying."

When you find yourself doing the lion's share of a long portage, do you react with a roar, or quiet pride?

    "Sorry, I wanted to see how you do it."

When the scouting canoe disappears, does it mean okay, come ahead, or yikes, pull in?

    "Sorry, I just got carried away."

When they fight over who gets to scrape the pot, is it a compliment to the cook?

    "Sorry, you're all growing so quickly."

When some red-breasted Loriens go bob-bob-bobbing down a bouncy stretch of white water, can we successfully pretend that we're not staring?

    "Sorry, I thought you were a boys camp."

When the excitement of a moose splashing at the bend ahead turns out to be two birthday-suited Loriens, should we pretend disappointment?

    "Sorry, I thought you were a moose."

When your fellow paddler goes on a singing jag, "Oh my boot lash busted, uh oh oh, ho ho"... or you're paddling with a pathetic versifier, "I'm wheezin' 'cause I'm freezin', it's the season, and I'm kneelin' on my knees, an' it ain't pleasin', but I'm F-R-E-E to stop and P-E-E---." Aren't you lucky?

"Indian carvings! <u>Recent</u> ones!"

"If you want good food, go to the Hilton."

"We're doing all this for...fun?"

"Catch and Release. Forget it! This can of tuna
    has all the protein of a big minnow."

"He bit through the steel leader, and that's my lure
    there, below.

That pike is fishing...for me!"

Rules for a Rainy Morning

Tighten fly ropes only when you finally just can't put off any longer going out to pee.

Let morning's fire be made by whoever can no longer wait for a cup of coffee.

Rise only with the barometer.

Listen to the pitter–patter, the clucking grouse, the impervious loons; don't listen to the mosquitoes.

Let the weather make up your mind; in other words, turn over and go back to sleep.

If you're in love with your tent mate, pray for a sustained deluge.

On a Cold Night

She gathers all the blankets –––
It's her trick
To make me cuddle close
        (Or end up sick.)

I pretend I'm unaware
Of her technique,
Because I love her
Right down to my warming feet.

Wilderness Disconnect

Overloaded
With gear, and guile,
They dumped, but not quite alone.
Overheard, screaming,
Panicky pleading,
"The phone, save the phone, the PHONE!"

The Empty Insides

Where terra firma still defies,
We fly through waves and sail the skies.

Twelve thousand natives paddled here
Before we came with our awesome gear.

In a chopped–out tree they tackled whales.
We get miffed if the weather fax fails.

Even Better Than the Mini-Mall Gym

It's harder
Portaging a canoe
In Ontario

Than climbing
With a 30 pound pack
Across the Alps.
But who's complaining?

Glistening alpine crests have their valleys...
A chef in every inn,
Handcrafted beers,
And featherbeds.

While spruce-scented northern trails
Lead to nurturing lakes,
Aboriginal campsites,
Dinners self-caught.
And we seek only the favor of the wind.

In the Alps we speak of Canadian sunsets
                    and glowing coals.
In Ontario we fondly replay Alpine glories.
Scramblers, and voyageurs
Reflecting youthful strengths
                    and pleasures.
Earth's beauties beckon......
And keep us young.

One Watch for Two Boats

"Did you tie up your boat?"
"Yep, tied it to yours."
Only "yours" wasn't moored to the shore.

Tied neatly together,
Then blown off by the wind,
We're suddenly transport poor.

Marooned, dismal thought,
With each other forever
To see our canoes nevermore.

T'was too much for Big Frank
Who with watch and clothes
Dived off with a splash and a roar.

Soon all reappeared
To our cheers and relief,
The tow line in Big Frank's mouth.

"A hero, oh no;
To be stuck here with you,
I'm a coward who just wanted out."

A Gift of Timex

I looked at my watch ---
Its digital face gone blank.
The end of time. Hooray!

Dropping all, we paddled to the nearest island
And no further.
Swam, ate, rested,
A timeless day.

Fish circled.
Dragon flies hovered.
Loons called, creating echoes,
We found faces in the clouds.

This morning the watch is working again.
Get up.
Move out.
Move on.

Mince on Mints

On our first family canoe trip, I brought mints to assuage a three year old's moments of challenge. Such as making it across to a point.

"Thank you!" Then, to the next point.

"Mint first."

"Hard, mint again."

"Two mints first."

"'Nother mint, *now*!"

"Can't go without 'nother mint."

"Three mints, now....*please*."

So no more mints. On future trips the subject never came up again. Going was its own reward. Until years later, with grown men on a tough portage, "Have a mint" became a long remembered boost.

"Sorry, Daddy,
For the time it takes
Because of all
My cuts and aches."

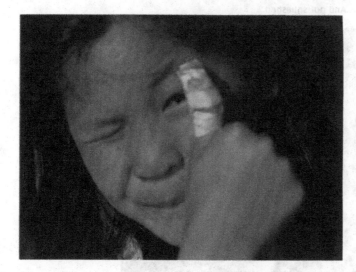

....Sores and stiffness,
Cramps, scratches, shakes,
Dings, bangs and bruises,
Bites, burns and scrapes,

...From traveling through
These peaceful lakes.

Bug Hero

In the night the bug bit
And I banged him hard;
Woke the dog with a start
And she barked;

Then the loons, now aroused,
Became wailers and howlers,
Scaring off prowlers
Of the dark.

So by morning our cache
Was still safely intact,
All was quiet, the threat
Had been quashed.

Thanks be to the biting
Bug hero, and martyr
Who set off the alarm
....And got squashed.

Like Chopsticks

We washed the dishes nicely
After a super sup,
And rinsed them oh so thoroughly
Especially this cup.

How Much Do I Love You?

It mattered not that our tent was askew.
A wind sock, oh no; she wanted a view.
So it angled uphill, and sagged in the middle,
No place in a downpour for water to dribble.

"So what if it rains and we get a bit wet?"
Our entrance net frames the forthcoming sunset.
Who needs room for the head? Align for the eyes
Exactly to catch the morning's sunrise.

So we pitched on a rain—cupping rocky ridge....
Perfect for black fly, mosquito and midge.....
Pretended to sleep between rocks in a rut;
Now have glacial striations all over my butt.

After You Gladly

At nine A.M. on July 28th
We finally found the first
Of the Sinton Creek portages....
Totally overgrown.
We were the season's first paddlers.

Starting at trailhead, we cleared the way,
Cutting branches, rolling and chopping deadfalls,
Our Lab panting back and forth,
Pioneers and adventurers breaking through!

At 10 A.M. on July 28th
At the end of the newly opened Sinton Creek portage,
Suddenly, as we were finally about to launch our canoes,
A black Lab appeared...but not our own...
Followed by....the second canoeing party of the season.

Nattily unsweated and unscratched
They brushed by, uncharacteristically self-absorbed,
Quickly putting in and pushing off.

We let them.

They might enjoy being pioneers for the
Next four portages ahead.

Board Meeting

When the trip was almost over
We judged it to be:

Too strenuous
Not strenuous enough
Too much time spent on fishing,
But not enough fish
Not enough time camping at beautiful places
Too much time "wasted" at certain campsites

There were differing opinions on
Whether vanilla pudding constitutes breakfast;
Whether to take so many bags of sunflower seeds,
     but no veggies;
Whether to again take prunes,
      which knocked out everyone except the cook;
Whether to again take the cook.

When we got home
We found it impossible
To settle down to anything.
The perfect trip.

Definition

Wilderness, heck,
Is where you can pee
Without wrecking your neck
Checking someone should see.

Urination Ruminations

Thy cascade so mighty,
My surge so small
As I humbly match streams
By Thy waterfall.

Not all wisdom's from
Deep rumination;
Inspiration can flow
From a urination.

Last Stop

When you're out to pee
On a summer night
Be sure to face north
For the Northern Lights.

But should the wind blow
From the north perchance
Be satisfied with
A backward glance.

Calm water reflects
A world often missed,
To which I add stars
When into it I've pissed.

Outdoor Pissibilties

We honor the civilities
In the absence of facilities
As the bushes and the backs of trees
Become our new pissilities.

Never on a trail, or site
As you bare your itty-bitty
Most discreetly out of sight,
And never in the city.

Some people seem always to have the wind with them,
Others know how to wait out the wind they need.
For some, no wind is the best one might hope for.
Me? I just break wind everywhere I go.

<u>Alexander the Grate</u>

There's Gregory the Beneficent
And Suleiman the Magnificent
But it was Dudley (the Salamander)
Who named our grill "Alexander"...
"You know, Alexander the Grate.".
And the coffee pot he called "Elmer"...
"Elmer's Perkin'!"

So now the knife is called "Mack",
As in "Mack the Knife",
And the outhouse is "Winnie"
As in Winnie the you know...who.
There is no single "Mr. Wonderful" on this trip.
Every guy quietly knows that he's...."the Magnificent".

He can't
Hear you,
He's walking
On the water.
Sure, he's using
A canoe.....
But only
As a starter.

You've got to give up snoozin'
If your bones are going cruisin';
Slowly, starting strokes revive...
Then bang! You're off in overdrive.

Invitation to a Secret

That special place was awfully nice.
Now paddlers galore it's got.
Promoted as a paradise,
Increasingly it's not.

    The continent's best known canoeing area
    Has a million canoe–able acres.
    Our neck of the Ontario woods has four million.

    The popularized place draws 200,000 paddlers a year.
    We hardly see 10,000.
    That's a people–pressure ratio of eighty to one, Yes 80!
    Eighty times greater than Ontario's equally compelling rivers, lakes and forest.

    So that other place, continuing subject of articles, now requires reservations,
    Against quotas,
        with entry dates,
            entry gates, and
                mandated exits.

    "Our" wilderness still beckons...quietly.
        Come when,
            stay where, and
                as long as you wish.

Ticketron wilderness really pissed her.
Lakes as God made them deserve but a whisper.
"So whisper, just where
Is your smugly special place?
I'm guessing Algonquin....
Is that your paddling base?"

No...nor is it Wabakimi,
In northwest Ontario
With 5,000,000 acres for 800 paddlers.
Try the math on that one!

"Somewhere in–between?"
YES.

Canoe and Kayak Trails

Rivers, first trails,
Linked waterways, used and abused
Emerging clear and redeemed,
Resuming their natural effulgence.
Returning to the paddler,

More access, new put-ins, portages reopened,
Campsites established
From Canada and Maine to Florida,
Puget Sound north,
And in-between coast to coast.

Old trails reopened, new trails created,
Invitational, unobstructed, protected exploring,
Legalized, subsidized and officially sanctified cruising.

So go for it!
And if you can't join the trail blazers or the keepers,
Thank the dedicated promoters, clubs, and yes, a spirited paddlesport industry
For easing us onto the water.

Motherships

Mothers

Love you ($200 a day)

Nurture you (Who's doing breakfast?")

Indulge you ("There's no more hot water.")

Teach you ("Your skirt's on backwards.")

Protect you ("It poured last night.")

Enforce discipline ("Mother's not coming. We paddle BACK.")

Promote family ("All of our wine is homemade.")

Build character ("So, glacial rinse water IS cold.")

Establish limits ("Ve VILL stay together ven ve are on MY trip.")

Punish the wayward ("All those whales. No time for tea.")

Not all mothers are created equal, but all that we have experienced
are remembered with affection. All offered the best.

Big Mothers

Who doesn't love a mother?

    Mothers enable

    Mothers nurture

    Mothers protect

    Mothers coddle

    Mothers help us see, explore, engage, and appreciate the world around us.

    Yea, Motherships!

    If only those mothers didn't charge.....

PORTAGING

Some pronounce it PORTage,
As in water shortage.

Others call it porTAGE
As in blue trail mirage.

I carry my canoe,
My canoe carries me.
It's easier by far
For it than for me.

Nature's ways
Sometimes seem perverse
When its pleasures are granted
From things in reverse.

After four million years
Of physical struggle,
Our systems resent
A perpetual cuddle.

Portages
Could never
Be billed
As great fun.

Rather,
They're bills
To be paid
On the run.

They're an
Unblemished show's
Simple price
Of admission.

Your receipt
Is a sore
But improved
Condition.

Full of life they were not,
They looked totally shot,
Of pain did complain;
But all talk.
For they rose from the dead
When the master said,
"Pick up thy canoe,
And walk."

<u>Been There</u>

Ugh, push...
Ankles in moosh.
Sore arms,
Tired tusch.

Twist, lift,
Bumps and knocks,
Scrapes and scratches,
Sadistic rocks.

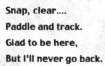

Snap, clear....
Paddle and track.
Glad to be here,
But I'll never go back.

I carried their canoe,
Will they carry mine?
Will they want to go, still?
Will I?

Little hands on large paddles,
Fresh minds recording
Routines as pleasures;
Events, lasting treasures.

They struggled, full of faith,
I watched them grow.
Will I struggle, keep the faith,
And still grow as I go?

The Last Portage

Planing home on overly solicitous waves
From a southwest summer wind
That roars above, and through the tops of the tallest trees,
An invisible force in a cloudless sky,
The dot ahead becomes.....
Our dock
Stable amidst the smashing foam.
We unload, carrying gear up to the cabin
....The last portage.

We have climbed the last portage many times;
With the children since they were four,
Once in a driving late August sleet, trail coated in ice,
Tired muscles drawn to refuge and rest.

Canoe trips end, a convergence of feelings,
But the last portage,
Thoughts of cold drink or hot mug,
Familiar bed, clean sheets, deferred desires,
Contrasts, the old made new,
Easily draw us uphill to the welcoming hearth.

The Last Portage II

Final strokes to the familiar dock,
Canoes out,
 Everything swiftly up hill, open the door, and
 The cabin appears cavernous,
Emptier,
Too clean to trod?
 Is that a bathroom scale?
What day is it?

The bags, color-coded, so carefully packed,
Carelessly disgorge dirty laundry, pine needles,
 Ending the focused simplicity,
 The hallowed clarity.

 Over stimulating alien sights and sounds,
While the body still feels the swells and miles.

 The dog stretches,
Stands briefly,
Curls back into her favorite place,
A good example.

Temagami, Laced and Linked

Who has walked this trail before me,
Traced by prowling beasts
And aborigines since the glacial recession?

We know this oxbow cut was dug by the hands of Temagami Ned.
The cliff of this Cree portage was defiantly painted by an Iroquois war party.
How many European explorers came this way?
Who moved those rocks? Voyageurs?
Trappers? Hudson Bay men? Priests?
Prospectors? Loggers? Firefighters? Fishermen?

We know these trails are as old as human life in the area;
Ten thousand years at least.
And that this region alone has over twelve hundred portages,
All recorded in their native names
As a labor of love by Craig McDonald.

Portages: some summer, some only winter, some popular, some strategic,
Witnesses to man's two–footed history.
Warriors, carriers of faith, furs, fire pumps, precious hopes of ore,
Did all by paddling
And placing of one foot before the next.

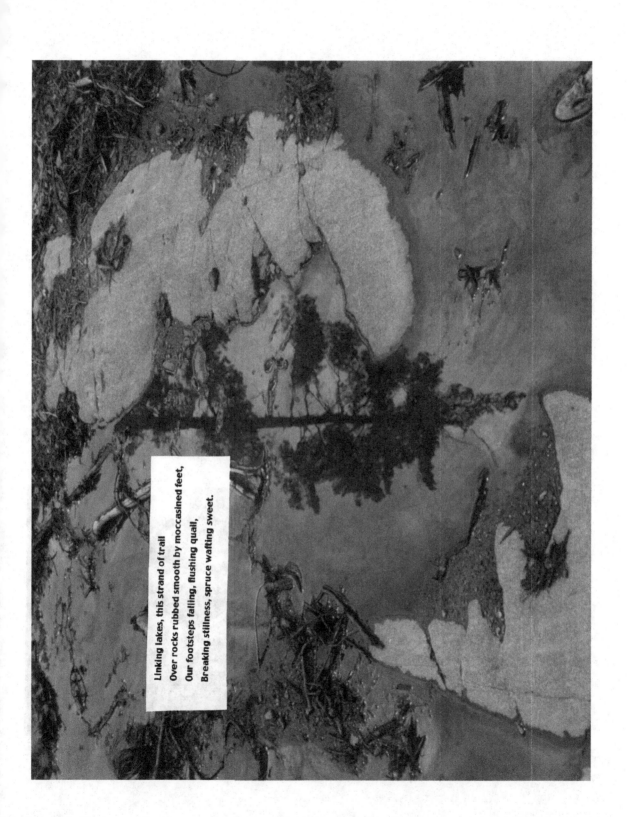

Linking lakes, this strand of trail
Over rocks rubbed smooth by moccasined feet,
Our footsteps falling, flushing quail,
Breaking stillness, spruce wafting sweet.

She'd confirm and scout
Every portage for us'n
Which spared us a lot of
Discussion and fussin'.

The Alluring Lure of a Choice Insecure
(Let Sloping Logs Lie)

A sloping log,
When portage foot–sloggin',
Is a tricky dog fraught
With knocks for the noggin.

Any angled log
Is bound to be ....
Like an underfoot frog....
Quite slippery.

The fate for flirtation
By stepping off too often
May be a date
In an ornate (wood) coffin.

"Child's play," you say,
With a carefully put foot,
Slither.....sliding away,
Landing canned, kaput.

"I'm cautious as sin,
But this one's okay,"
And another limb meets
Its judgment day.

Face it, such falls
From logs are myriad,
We just won't step on such
A log again, period!

Crash!!
Damn.

The "Portage Store"

I've been blessed with so much more...
All praises for the "Portage Store".

Old socks and jocks I can ignore
But not good shoes, or a fine drill core.

A sweater that some brambles tore,
Perfect boots the Dutch prince wore.

Cups, caps, ax, some copper ore,
Sometimes a very fine fishing lure.

Oh yes, we've left behind our share,
To dwell on that I do not dare.

A voyager out of Hibernia
Paddled in the noon sun; that'll learn ya.
It'll burn ya and turn ya
Without a hat, durn ya ---
To a voyageur-bright red sunburnya.

This very same man from Hibernia
Decided to portage on his journey a
Hundred pound pack
Without heart attack ---
Stumble-bumbled his bundle to a hernia.

COOL!!!

The...

END

MUG & GRUB

Our Favorite Gourmet Chef

Guys tend to be better with the mug than the grub.

Most men, when charged with preparing a cookfire dinner, are an unpredictable quantity. Even when competent at home, whether as fussy gourmet chef or king of the grill,...still one never knows what to expect, in rotation, from the designated cook. Out on the trail they are saved only by the grace and ravenous appetites of their buddies. At such times the term "buddies" may be stretching things a bit. Most of the bellyaching that follows is from men having to eat the cooking of other men. Meanwhile,our kids, having learned from over the wood coals, could out cook most of the guys. But one of the most experienced expedition paddlers of all, from Canadian Shield to Arctic, lived largely on oatmeal and tea.

Many Midden Mouthfuls

How many elders sat right here,
Before i reached this place?
Each shell a midden mouthful....
i'm just the latest feeding face.

Where are the midden maidens?
Where gone a thousand belles?
This lunch of ours preceded by
Their hundred million shells.

A Part-Timian

I'm a summer Indian
With paddle an amphibian;
A proud part-time Canadian,
And skunked, a vegetarian.

The Pancake That Changed the World

Well, our world anyway.

The well-intentioned fathers-sons canoe trips lacked nothing, except.....well, we needed a woman...well, not because she was beautiful, but because she was beautiful and could cook.

So we voted, no glass ceilings in these woods.

Of course, it changed the culture, this switch from big and little Macho Men to coed and, of course, it was well worth it.

As for that historic sourdough pancake – it made a nice frisbee.

The CHAMP!

She could sniff at all those outdoor cookery books that just assumed refrigeration and electricity.

Our luck..... she had learned from some of those simple cookfires shared by traditional peoples in other corners of the planet.

The food dehydrator humming away each spring was able to dry just about anything. Well, the tuna was a bit rubbery and spinach a no-go.

The component of a balanced meal in little zip-lock bags came together in a larger meal-size zip-lock bag, with each meal identified, then packed in eating order.

On a fourteen day trip she managed meals for four out of a single rec pack. That's 168 meals... and if that weren't enough, there were no complaints, only compliments. We added occasional fish. Dried hamburger would be re-hydrated by placing it in a quart jug with water early in the day. By supper time it would be completely resurrected.

Oh yes, Northwoods paddlers know where to find water.

B.C. (Before Coffee)

If I start the day
Rather grumpily,
Thank you at least
For my company.

****

The geese out there are squawking.
Screaming gulls have taken wing.
Even seals are barking.
Coffee me, and I will sing.

Regal mug of coffee in
My warm nesting bed.
Dripping down towards ignition....
Growing hope for my head.

Blue berries....
    A canoe trip's commas,
    Periods,
    Occasional exclamation points.

Who can paddle past blueberries?
    "We're bursting ripe,
    Just waiting for you, big boy."

From blessing of berries so propitious...
We gobble up pancakes so nutritious.
Letting good fortune so delicious
Outweigh grubby hands so inauspicious.

Acceptable Nationalism

Blueberries, raspberries,
Hidden pearl snowberries,
Juicy gems of the trail,
Fresh with dew.

Dawn's promise and fragrance
Fill begging tin cup....
Sweet cheers for the
Red, white and blue.

A Fastidious Camper's Non-Saturated Oil Emergency Shaving Mirror

Wilderness mirror for fried fish and meat
Gazing is nice, but when can we eat?

When They're Biting.....

From breakfasts through suppers
We shaked and baked,
And baked and ate,
And ate and ate.

Then fried and poached,
Even boiled and broiled,
Fish burgers, fish soufflé,
Chowder, cake, consommé.

With butter, with sauces,
From juicy to tender,
From smoky to mooshy
.....But never sushi.

With waves I connive,
I struggle, and strive
To survive and arrive
For your cocktails at five.

No wind's bluster and commotion
Nor tempestuous ocean motion
Curb our dutiful devotion
To the evening's hot rum potion.

That Gawdawful Lousy Stew...Again

"Whatdy you mean 'It's All Gone?!!!"

Trip Food Confidential

Comparisons with past repasts
From gourmet dining to deli's,
Chow hounds seem never to have enough
As they shamelessly stuff their bellies.

Food touched by repellent
Becomes an expellant.
Your tantalizing stew with its heavenly scent
Becomes our latest flatulent.
But those bakery bought strudels beat oodles of noodles
And sweetly promote canoeing canoodles.

Faddish diets from multimedia
Can't compare with "just don't eatia."

The diarrhea diet works
For folks as well as moose:
Let the juice of the spruce
Keep you running and loose.

People are no threat
When their needs are met.....
So hustle up the grub,
It's high time we et.

"Where the hell's
The son of a witchin'...

Who's been messin'
In my kitchen?"

Rain is but water....
Wind's nothing but air....
Riled up, agitated
A most cussed pair.

One's body itself
Is but water and air
Disrupted again
Since beans 'bin our fare.

If I paddle real good
It's not thanks to the food.

Which gentleman voyageur

?!

Was the cook?

<u>Oh No, Not the Pot</u>

James
Loves the North...

The paddling,
The poeting,
Yes, the portaging.

But twists into knots
Over blackened pots.

Sometimes of necessity,
One must read the recipe.
Our last concoction raised a stench,
Because the English part got soaked,
And the rest was French.

How to Cook a Recipe

1) Dissolve in water.

2) Add for flavor.

Alone Together

Sweet mystery, your recipe
For ecstasy, with misery.
No other dish quite stirs me
Like your gut expanding chili.

No one now dare come between us
With whatever noble intent
While we're suffering together
In this small enclosing tent.

Jack is chopping bullfrog legs
To be fried with scrambled eggs.

Still I get a bit uptight
When breakfast twitches with each bite.

And I'd much prefer my lunch
Not to wiggle as I munch.

My favorite meal is supper
When it doesn't come back upper.

(A fantasy, and dated. Today's bullfrogs have earned more respect, even names like "Mr. Charlie". We leave them be, subject only to "Mr. Raccoon", "Mr. Blue Heron", "Mr. Pike".)

News is hot.
(Coffee's not.)

A Missed Supper Night's Dream

Blew my nose
And it woke up the forest.

Then I sneezed
And it brought up the sun.

Coughed and felled
Low–flying roast ducks.

Pulled in
A fried trout just for fun.

FISHIN' & WISHIN'

Of course you can cruise without a fishing rod. But back country angling for many is the icing on the cake. With access to waters seldom visited, quiet gliding over aquarium visibility makes for "fishing" with or without a pole. Actually you can troll on the way to your campsite with just a line and lure off the stern. Light collapsible rods are more sporting, and for the dedicated fanatic there are specially designed craft that offer more comfort and stability when casting for the big ones.

Definitions:
"Catch and Release" means
Releasing yourself from carrying back,
Decapitating,
Gutting, cleaning, filleting,
Cooking, cleaning, and carefully
Disposing of all remains.

This method is preferable to:
"Catch and Early Release",
Wherein the decision for release
is entirely the fish's,
Sometimes even before you've
figured out what you had on.

The Little Girl Hustle

She caught the silvery giant
By hustling out of a cozy warm bag
Before any other.

Propelled by excitement
The older sleepyheads tumbled forth in quest
---- As if there could be another.

Recession

Line Dancing

It was muggy
And buggy,
We dozed...
It was late...

Hydraulic
Explosion!
He'd taken my bait.

Galvanized...
Electric...
I played him
Sublime.

Snap!
Final triumph!
His.
Not mine.

Wishin'

It's such hard work,
This fishin'
When your catch is based
On wishin'

Especially when,
With grand hauteur,
They casually bump
Aside your lure.

Stringer empty...
No addition,
I shall return...
I vow attrition!

One More Excuse

When blissfully suspended
In the ethereal,
Bites become
Immaterial.

"No fish up there, Daddy."

Not for the Taking

Thunder and lightning
Bearing down in a rush
Just when action
Teases my lure.

Cursing, then dashing
Reluctantly
I race to pull
Up on the shore.

Dream interrupted....
No fish fillet lunch...
As I scrunch under
My turned–over canoe.

When next to my shelter
By edge of lake
A many–meals monster
Rises to view....

A leviathan giant
Casually there where I lie
Nonplussed and staring
As if to say "Hi!"

Startled, I fixate,
Both helpless and peeved,
A fish never seen,
Nor to be believed.

Then my breathless farewell
To this creature revealed
As he dives to the deep....
And perhaps back to sleep?

Gone forever, an apparition
Not to be caught or to munch.
Ephemeral, awesome, and besides...
He could have had me for lunch.

You, Me, Them

We rose, returning "Sam Peabody's" call,
Paddled grey-red waters,
Portaged upcountry, sun breaking,
A day's fishing trip.

Perfume of sweetgrass and spruce,
Coffee on the trail,
We put in, shoreline emerging,
Mirrored beyond the dissolving mist.

Our eyes touch bottom; then ripples,
Gentle gusts, clearing skies,
Paddling past breezy points into quiet bays,
Casting under rock faces glacially etched.

Alone
Together
Memories of other times
Here
Elsewhere
You
Me
No bites.

Point of View

Little can of tuna,
Having logged thousands of miles,
And now paddled and portaged to this northern shore,
Its raison d'etre, its moment;
The grand opening!

Grateful I should be, to have it here
Because I didn't pull in any keepers.
Yet my rejected catches could have filled two dozen teeny tuna cans
For a luncheon dish
Much more delish.

Time Zones

He rose early
As did I, with the sun.

Paddling,
I passed him on the dock.

As I began casting
He started across the lake.

By seven he was on the mainland,
By nine in the air,
Ten o'clock....Toronto.

He, winging his way to Europe,
I'm still trying for my first fish.

His lunch...over the Atlantic
When I finally caught "breakfast",
Ate,
And caught up on my sleep.

Morning stillness.
Time suspended.
Silver flash!
Silence ended.

Didn't snag.
Didn't break.
Meter's running,
I'm awake.

The Heart of the Matter

"Catch and Release"
Gets you "hands halitosis"
While increasing your score for
Arteriosclerosis.

Fishing for Their Freezers

I try to keep secret
My favorite bass holes
From pernicious
Avaricious
Hoarding assholes.

Many Happy Returns

Three times he broke off
Just to come back for more;
When I caught him his mouth
Was a hardware store.

A Fish for All Seasonings

Fish for breakfast and for brunch,
Fish for dinner and for lunch,
Fish for hors d'oevres and PM snacks.
And dessert?......Heck, no, relax.

Flexible Leader-ship

Bass charging towards shore,
Zinging back in reactions,
Extra playing galore
Real rubber band action.

My leader did twist,
Stretch, wiggle and squirm.
It turned out to be
My blue plastic worm.

First Class

Smooth-grained cherry paddle.....
Gleaming golden day,
In sunshine's beams, living my dreams,
Perfect in every way.

Those affording simple tastes
Know the meaning of "first-class".
Worldly success ain't happiness,
Krugerrands, or bass?

Reeling In

Magical surroundings....
Splashing thoughts for the getting...
From a handsome canoe
In a northern lakes setting.

"No strikes" is a strike-out
For quite a few guys.
Some get fish.
Others get wise.

No Bait? No Problem! No Fish.

Our finest fish getter
Left the worms on the shore.
But this champion forgetter
Showed he knows how to score.....

He used a chance frog
To catch him a bass.
Reused the chewed sog
To catch them en masse.

Then one of the livelies
Coughed forth a crayfish
Which landed a whopper
Beyond fondest wish.

Thus catching the limit,
We could handle no more
(Not needing the worms
Left forgotten on shore.)

But our prize-winning
Fish–catching champion forgetter
Then forgot to top knot
His catch any better.

And while turning back home
His large lively stringer
Sailed away with a flourish
.........Spaghetti for dinner.

Wet Dreams

When from a deep sleep
You hear grinding of teeth
And your fisherman moans, groans and screams,

It's a sad day's replay
Of what got away
.....And you thought erotic dreams?

Buff's Lake

We fished all we wished,
Then we ate and ate,
Had it whole, fried and baked,
It was great.

Ate fish breaded and stuffed,
And with mayonnaise chilled;
No such thing as enough.
We thrilled, grilled and filled.

Filleted and poached our favorite dish
On this final night on shore.
Boy, oh boy, do we love fish?
No, not so much anymore.

Reciprocity
(A Fish Story)

Left canoe on shore to hop out and find
A retreat for my urgency.
But when I returned, sassy bass on my stringer
Were towing all out to sea
And jeering in chorus, "Catch and release!"
While wiggling their tails back at me.

So now heading back with my share
Of smallmouth wild and frisky,
My six-fish power motor tows me home.
Then of course, I set them all free.

The Involved Fisherman

He fished, and he fished,
And ate all he could eat
'Til one day he found out
He had flippers for feet.
......Another fish story.

The Naked Canoeist

Fishing on a wilderness lake
On a quiet, misty morning,
The silence shatters when,
Like a shot from around the point
An alien approaches;
"Where's the "!#" portage?"

Reveries interrupted.
Barbarous intrusion.
Yes, I'm miffed.
Accosted, I'm here to fish.
Besides, my good wife Judy does our social.

She points the way, turns back to me with a
       "Wow...How 'bout that!"
       "What?"
       "The girl. Gorgeous. And totally naked!"
       "Huh? I wasn't wearing my glasses."
So much for the fisherman's fantasy...how to catch a fisherman.
Skunked.
And I let my wife do the social.

Never leave your glasses at home.
And maybe your wife?

First Day

Landed one dozen bass
In retirement's glow.
Twice the limit
So I let six go.

Then, so the others
Might, like me, be free,
Let each slip the chain.
Total amnesty.

THE WILD SIDE

Slillies

Ducks and geese flying north
"On corth, of corth,"
Tailing their wags
Behind them.

One spring-flying flock
Heading south willy-nilly
Caused young Laurie to shout,
"Not that way, you slillies."

Summer North. Winter South

We're just like those ducks
.....Seasonal fliers,
Same destinations,
Only we fly on tires.

Young Survivors

As they paddle past the proud Mother Loon
Who is caring for a tiny Merganser chick,
Our kids understand.
They too were adopted.

                 ****

Observing the train of neatly– spaced skittering ducklings
Headed by Mighty Mother Merganser.
Little legs scrambling to keep up,
One feared for the last vulnerable chick,
A tempting bite for a hungry pike.
Suddenly – a roiling burst from below ---
Took down Mom.

Sea Otters

By day the males fight
And try to bite
Their rivals' competitive issue.

But together at night
They link arms oh so nicely
For some there's no longer an "issue".*

*But it can grow back.

Tough Love

In the quiet of autumn mist we paddle past
Four forms idly floating together.
Suddenly silence is broken by cries
And beating of wings against water.

Father loon lifts his white breast,
Spreads his wings wide, primed to fly.
Two small loons look on,
Fearful, protesting, hastily swim towards mother.
Suddenly both parents take off,
Abandoning their youngsters,
Who alarmed, struggle flapping across the smooth water,
Attempting to follow.

Parents swoop overhead, then
Wing off to the next inlet, while below
Slapping and screaming
With a surge of energy,
One youngster leaps free,
Sustaining momentum,
Lifting off, flying, free.
The other tires, fails.

On return we again pass four forms,
Adults silently gliding,
Offspring excitedly trilling.
September means fly or die.
Tough love though it be,
Leads to summer returns.

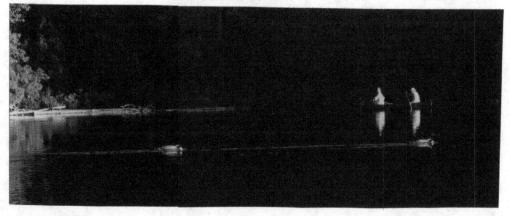

The Cosmopolitan

As our canoe nears, only one turtle,
Dignity intact, remains on the log.
The others all skitter off, plopping away
As we glide by.

This one turtle, who returns our gaze, once traveled far from here,
To be our children's pet.
But after three weeks he was returned
Back to his home base, here.

Each spring there he sits;
Grown a bit larger,
And still less frightened than the others.

This cosmopolitan has seen something of the world.
Confidently he stares back.
We're looking at a turtle with panache!

Friends of Humankind

The wrens had become quite friendly,
Having accompanied my summer efforts at clearing,
Thus netting themselves a steady supply of bugs.

Now, paddling home, we could hardly believe
The little parade that flitted and followed our canoe down the shoreline.

They were probably chirping,
    "Hey, come back."
But we preferred to think of it as
    "Farewell, and thanks."
            ****

Years later, leaving behind a friendly black bear, a similar farewell:
He had hung around all summer, and supplying food we definitely did not,
But we got to know and respect each other.
He followed our departure the length of the shoreline, until our kids said,
    "Look, he's waving good-bye."
And he was....up on his hind legs, probably balancing madly with his paws.
We preferred to think of it as
    "Farewell, and have a good hibernation."
            ****

The loon, that proudly brought by her chick to show off and share,
No question about that.

Earthquake at Spiderville – Web Exposed

While morning finds me slipping
Into water, off to roam,
Old "Biterman" there sits dripping mad;
I bumped and jarred his home.

"Jaws – First Spider

This delicate creation
Of divine design
Is really just a
Sign to dine.

But the hero of this
Seamless scene
Would, modest artist,
Rather not be seen.

His table all set
With sparkling crystal
"Jaws" awaits dinner
Blowing in on the "mistral".

"Grabber" – Second Spider

They call me "the Grabber",
For breakfast I jab–er,
Then stab'er and have 'er,
My gourmet cadaver.

Nature made me a zapper,
With no time to mourn'er
This isn't McDonald's
But not a bad corner.

"Chomper" – Third Spider

Silver strands blinking
Like a car dealer's lot.
Inconspicuous
It's not.

His trap made bright
With warning lights
Cheats "Chomper" out of his
Morning bites.

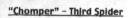

Taking Each Bite Personally

Put his faith in Deet
For the nightly slaughter,
Even tried going incognito;

But Dudley got carried
Away, bit by bit, by
Mosquito after mosquito.

Shower time

When the skeeters are scrambling
To abandon the tent
Heaven–sent message?
Or unheavenly scent?

Junior Draculas

Pesky critters
Bugger off!
As I roll my tent away.

You partied all night
On me....your host,
And now I'm too drained to play.

Junior Helicopters

Junior choppers
Roaring round my head
Chomping skeeters, disconcerting,
But it makes them dead.

Whale Tales

Alexandra Morton has written about hearing the engines of an oncoming ship, but unable to see (or be seen) in the fog, when a pod of orca appeared and shepherded her out of harm's way.

Another such incident was related to me by a canoeist who, with his partner, was ending a weekend paddle on the West Coast. Rounding a point to get back to their car, the wind had risen and the waves were tremendous. Only their need to be at work on Monday morning led them onward to risk a try. Just when they realized that they had no chance in the heavy seas, a whale appeared, placing itself close by, protectively on the seaward side. It accompanied them the entire kilometer of dangerous waters. As they safely reached the bay, the whale sounded and was not seen again.

Not confirmed, but a good story: Two loggers started their harvest sliding down seawards for towing. One was careful to avoid the transient orca below, the other went out of his way to aim for it....the log hit. He cheered his success. When done and in their boat heading home, the struck whale appeared, smashed into the boat, and successfully drowned only one logger, his tormentor.

His Nibs of the Mountain

HE...Regal Eagle..was soaring IN PLACE
As we met on His mountain, face to face.
A wingspread equal to my height, quivered slightly
Just feet away, only feet below the pinnacle.

He ...perfectly trimmed to the thermal.
Me...Breathing hard from a no-trail ascent.
He...Enjoying the updraft --suspended --- Mr. Cool.
We...both knew
He belonged here,
His peak.
Who was I?

He...In his own time, banked, glided away while
I...Retraced every awkward step; but that night
I..Slept in a cozy warm nest

                ...and dreamt of soaring.

Revelations

Lakes reveal
What's ahead
What's above
And sometimes what's below.

Lakes reveal
Oncoming winds
Strength of rising waves
While there's time to respond.

Lakes reveal
The lighter
As well as t he darker side of sky
Gentleness of evening
Against the fury of day.

Lakes reveal
The layered dome of an entire storm
Not just raindrops;
Endless forests
More than trees;
Lakes also reveal trees.

Lakes reveal
Nothing.....
If you look only ahead,
But direction
When looking ahead, to a distant shore.

Unsettled, a lake becomes an arena
For natural forces in conflict
And even the fish lie low.

Bring It On

We're not apt to notice
A wet epidermis
When the feel of a boat is
Pure bliss.

No dampening of fun
When an internal sun
Turns on, glows and shines
Limitless.

Cozy is nice
But weather adds spice,
Mother Nature's warm welcome
Wet kiss.

It does stand to reason
To dress for the season
Or that spice and that glow
Go amiss.

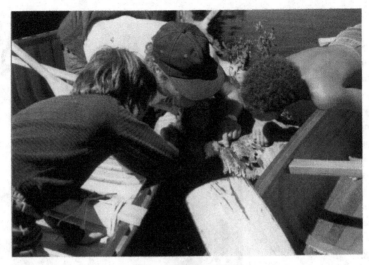

How 'Bout That

Nature eliminates the peripheral, the useless, the nonessential;
Nature balances, and sizes.

Nature focuses and concentrates;
Nature maximizes.

Nature's functional simplicity defines, distills,
Highlights and crystallizes.

Nature gives us meaning, beauty, life,
And sometimes tries us.

Maple Reminders

Red flags
That challenge dreams....
It is later
Than it seems.

Mind Snapping (Photographically)

The campfire was already blazing
Against the dull gray of a new dawn
When the sun peeked through, and over the trees.

Instantly turning the curling fog
Into pinks, oranges, yellows
Billowing over the gold
Then silver-etched canoe.

White swirls, like puffs from dry ice,
Gently circled the island beyond,
Ghost skaters in a huge arena.

Two loons, cutting V's
Came straight on with "Good morning's"
While a third skidded to a spectacular mist-parting landing.

Get the picture?
Because last night I ran out of film!

****

Three otters tumbled their way across to my shore
Playing at my feet as I cast.
One grabbed the bass on my line and swam off,
The others following and, yes, laughing.

You'll have to take my word for it.
I was still out of film.

****

A hawk that fell out of the tree,
And then walked down the road with me.
No camera.

****

The bear who wanted me to share
The fish on my stringer.
No time.

Count Me In

Spring! Exploding
Primal force!
(Including
You and me of course.)

Kids with Guns

I paddle past the noisy lair
Of mighty hunters of the bear.
They've flown up here for outdoor fun
--- Like killing dump bears on the run.

In camouflage costumes and smart lettered hats
They toy with their guns and imagine their splats.
With much macho talk (which we have to hear)
They down a few bear, but mostly beer.

Tossing their empties, and cigarette butts---
Gunning down "Yogis", the size of small mutts---
Displaying stuffed cubs-- that really takes guts ---
Oh, mighty hunter--- most glorious putz.

Some ranged the landscape for, not bear, but "foxes",
Lost all night on the lake (no streets or mailboxes).
These heroes then offered to *save* us from bear
"Overrunning the bush"---just not seen anywhere.

Someday they may, as they play, drink and cuss,
Shoot one another, thus ending the fuss.
"Harvesting" hunters would be a big plus,
'Cause bears are less trouble than hunters for us.

Hot Eco-Product

Yours for the gathering, dehydrated, light, odorless, as plentiful as acorns, but with lots more uses.

NORTHERN ALLURE – Boutique Size #1

Give your flowers a treat , to be sure,
With NORTHERN ALLURE, "The Chic Manure"
Of balsam balls and recycled spruce,
Produced for your use by Canadian moose.

Not moosh from the biggest tusch in the bush,
But yer delicate crisp-clean spherical pellet.
A renewable resource just going to waste....
Which is why we decided to save it and sell it.

From this lordly creature in forest ambiance,
Dehydrated to you, for your convenience.
It comes drop-shipped in a state unrefined,
Surely one of the greatest gifts of it s kind;

Give one to each plant (and add "one for the
                        pot"),
Generous portions guarantee a fine crop.
Aroma of forest may waft your way,
But not recommended for a closet sachet.

They'll start your fire on a rainy day,
Or just smolder, keeping mosquitoes at bay,
Serve as marbles with which the cat might
                        play,
While keeping the mice (and some neighbors)
                        away.

A dollar two dozen for NORTHERN ALLURE,
"The Chic Manure" by your cottage door,
The best friend old growth ever had
So, stocking stuffer for the boss, or Dad?

LOOSE MOOSE ** Valu~Pak #2

For special occasions try our VALU~PAK
Of LOOSE MOOSE MANURE from the beast with the rack.
Big jobs take a little more....
A little more money and lots more manure.

Serve up some real bush food to that dying tree
That's collapsing on your cottage in Temagami.
Put some in your neighbor's garden; Gee,
What a surprise for he (slash she).

Pile it on your trails in clumps neat and gritty
To impress those visiting guests from the city.
Reconstitute with water, to renew color and true scent,
Then excite those sleeping hunters plopping all before their tent.

If sunsets seem similar everywhere
Then let LOOSE MOOSE spruce up your twilight fare;
Its use in behalf of a foreground most fair
Will give all your sunsets that northern flair.

100% Canadian made...any profit we've got stays here.
Some we'll allot to preserving moose country....the rest goes to Moosehead beer.
You'll find these gems as you paddle and roam,
But first buy these (to cover my fees), then berry pail-go get your own.

Towering Monarch of the Forest Products Ltd. (very)

Nature's Bounty – SOLD OUT!

Who Owns the River?

The logger? The farmer?
The water company? The power company?
The mill?

The deer that drink at twilight?
The fishermen? The fish?
Paddlers? the poet?

Many users,
Some abusers.
Who owns the river?
None but the Giver.

"Where Have All the Rivers Gone?"

"Wild and Scenic Rivers" versus
60,000 dams...
600,000 miles of rivers drowned...
600,000 damns!

The Wild and Scenic Rivers Act
Saved half of one percent;
For every mile protected
Eighty-five are dead and spent.

Of "wide Mo's" 2500 miles
Only 149 still flow.
The "Mighty Columbia" no longer moves,
The Colorado's a Pacific no-show.

Killing rivers costs us all,
Anyone asking "Why?"
Chief Seattle's answer: "HOW
Can you buy or sell the sky?"

Whose Rights?

It's MY wilderness says the fisherman, the hunter , the camper, the paddler.

It's really MINE says the guide, the bush pilot, the homesteader, summer cottager,
tourist operator.

It's MY wilderness, obviously, says the trapper, the prospector, the logger, the
miner, the surveyor.

It's MY wilderness, legally, says the ranger.

It's MY wilderness, my birthright, says the indigenous native.

It's my wilderness, for your salvation, says the artist, the tree hugger, the
researcher, the ecologist, the poet.

Where's MY wilderness? , asks the forest and its creatures.

Beauty contested
By the Midas touch ---
"Never enough" versus
"Always too much".

Calls for multiple use,
Cries of "I'll hear nonesuch,"
"Caw~caw," says the raven,
"It's time we go 'Dutch'."

Back to the Future

All woodsmen love trees,
Sometimes to a cause;
Some swing paddles,
Others --- saws.

Both hunter and logger
Once knelt before their quarry,
"Selective and renewable"
Beats "slaughtered" and "sorry."

Don't Log This Hugger

How dare I condemn
The logger's caper
When all I write is
Borne on paper.

For me not to see
Would be perverse.
It takes a tree
To free my verse.

"But It Is Not Nice?"

Dirk, visiting from Germany,
Nervously placed his rock
On top of the pile
Blockading the illegal road,
Each rock a passing paddler's protest.

Today he knows pride.
His rock, added to the others,
Stopped forever the destructive intrusion,
Saved forever a First Nation's homeland,
Preserved a wilderness.

Just Add Local Water, A Few Fish, and Very Berry Desserts

These smooshed cans and plastic bags
Are the TOTAL trash brought out
From a five–day, three adults plus three kids
Eighty–meals (many miles) canoe trip.

Home–dehydrated foods
(There's no shortage of water)
Make for an easier in,
And even easier out.

Something to shout about?

STUMP SERMONS

You're not
.....Stroke.....
Going to move "heaven and earth"
.....Stroke.....
Until you move
.....Stroke.....
Yourself.

Paddling's a matter of direction,

And balance;

Like life.

Nature may be impersonal,
But thank God for the spectacle.
Without denying the empirical,
Be sure to enjoy the miracle.

Options

Instead of working on this canoe,
I could be paddling it.

Sometimes......
When we do things that lead
To something special,
We could be doing that special something.

Sometimes.....
When we seek an independent life-style,
That's what we get....A style
Rather than an independent life.

Sometimes.....
When we look for another place,
We find "where" is not so important
As "what".

Sometimes......
Another place makes sense
Only if we can't do "it" where we are.
But aren't most things a function, not of place,
But of us?

Which is why I'm working on this canoe.
And then,
Grab a paddle!

Before Your Arms Drop Off

Each forward dip
The end draws near.
The time is now,
The future here.

Why put off Belize,
The Barrens or the Bay
Beyond that point of no return
Where strength has slipped away?

We're taught to save,
To restrain, to defer....
Sometimes from home, church and school.
But we can awake
And question, "Why wait?"
And defer the deferring. Cool!

Fortuity

Struggle, build security
To what stage of maturity?
Life's like an annuity.
So savor your fortuity.

Futurity

From working to living
He never switched tracks.
Now he lies there secure;
It's the living he lacks.

A gorgeous canoe
Doesn't promise you
"Can do".

A free lifestyle
Is something less than
An independent life.

'Til by Father Time Dismissed

Our abundance is....frustration,
This debilitating wait;
Never-ending obligations....
Versus let's be done and off, damn straight!

Lists, the glut, the duplications,
The obsessive object sate,
Draining weight on our relations....
Expiate! Eliminate!

From convention and dull habit,
Convenience and trite fashion,
It's time for felt commitments and
The focus of our passion.

There's no more time for everything.....
What's tops on your wish list?
Try dropping all for something,
'Til by Father Time dismissed.

Flip Side

With every kind of challenge
It's the getting back that counts.
One can do most anything.
But first price out that wayward fling....

Yes, one can do most anything
If it's not the push for everything.
Once, perhaps, you could do this AND that.
More often now, it's this OR that.

This, or that?
How great to choose.
Beats retreat into numbing booze,
And better than eternal snooze.

Remember Sundays?

First, intrigue and laughs – the comics,
Then Sunday school,
They're singing "Follow the gleam"...
I'm hearing "Follow the stream."
God always showed up in the afternoons,
By a flowing river.

So Now I Just Start Earlier

With zeal I steal off on Sundays,
To kneel in my canoe;
And slyly try
To solemnify
My high in Thy floating church pew.

The Reverse of Perverse

Great fun paddling,
Struggling against wind isn't so,
But, from pushing big wind.....
Paradise!

Picking raspberries is fun,
Except for those sneaky stickers
(And sticky sneakers)
But prickles net nectar.

For hot and sweaty....
Drink and dive into
Clear, bubbly champagne waters.

Cold...A cheery blaze; tired....
That blissfully snug fluffed-up sleeping bag.

Fishing's fun,
But like that pike,
Life is full of bones;
Drawing us beyond the bones, flip side of promise...
      Raspberries,
      Champagne,
      Huggery, snuggery,
      Savory pike,
Paradise!

A Good Paddling "Never Hurt Nobody"

From high-powered job
To chopping wood,
Or paddling each stroke
Frees up thoughts great and good.

Needing no Zen master,
No trip to Japan,
An ax or a paddle
Frees up the man.

Which Way?

Wealth can
Create Beauty
But what
Is Wealth?

Often it's fashioned
From time,
Youth and health.

Life tends to reward
The giving of self

With objects:

Or meaning:

Which way
Your wealth?

Wealth

Wealth is
What right now you've got.
Everything else
And elsewhere it's not.

Wealth is not
What you might, or could,
But what you're absorbed in.
So make it good.

There's a time for hoping,
Coping, referring,
But doing is better
Than deferring.

A life of richness
Rather than riches
Leave scrapping and grabbing
To the sons of witches.

Frost's "Back out of all
This now too much for us"
Costs nothing but
A retreat form the fuss.

Consciously focused,
Thriving without a qualm,
Frees up that "inner source
Of clarity and calm".

Thoughts for the Turkey Who Tossed Me with His Wake

Does a guy who sinks all he's got
Into his boat
Stay awake on stormy nights worrying
If it's staying afloat?

Does a guy whose boat costs 272 times more
Than mine
Have a 272 times better-than-me
Good time?

Do boating jokes about money-sucking water holes,
And a guy's two happiest days,
Build sympathy and support for when he
Goes for a raise?

Does a guy who spews carbons
From a boat that looks like a car
Measure his pleasure in
How fast , not how far?

When the "pleasure boat"'s taken
Your whole ball of wax,
Is it still a pleasure?
Can you relax?

The Ultimate Simplification

Floating free upon my back
Looking out beyond the sky
Soaking in uncluttered peace
Born of struggles to simplify.

To qualify for this blissful state
To get here to this hidden lake
Required desire and push and drive
Not your usual "piece of cake".

Simplicity springs from stringent controls,
Effort brings effortlessness,
Peace blossoms from out of the struggle.
Joy from the task and the quest.

Wrap up at work, close down the house,
Buy, supply, drive, park and shuttle,
Open cabin, then prepare to paddle....
Refit, secure cabin, outfit, and trip...

Paddle off, then portage,
Moving northward more and more.
Camp after camp, lake after lake
Till craft and clothes lie on the shore.

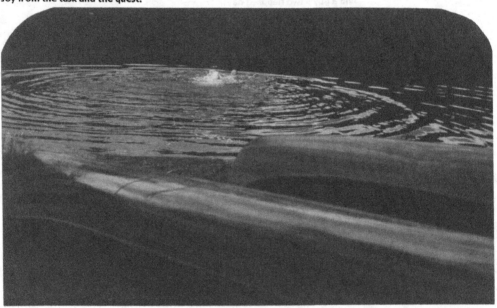

××××××××

And now I'm suspended in nothingness,
In clear water reflecting the sky,
Reluctant to splash the first shoreward stroke,
Afloat and wishing not to move....why?

That first stroke back to solid shore
.....Hearing echoes of Thoreau's cry....
Reverses the process, back to everyday stress
Unless there's success to simplify.

Beyond the Preachers

       (Lies the Greatest Teacher)

They dot Thy i's
And cross holy t's
And pretend to know
Thy will for me.

Like tiny droplets
Toward one great sea
May my conscious strokes
All lead to Thee...

Paddling untrammeled wildness
That bespeaks the Divine;
Resting awestruck beneath
Thy cathedral pine...

Fools lay claim
To Thy great plan;
While I wonder why
Thou should fool with man.

Beyond the Fog

Scientists tell us "what"
When what I want to know is "why",
Neither "how to" or "what for" deal with
The "Big What" beyond the sky.

Preachers, priests, the Pharisees
Spout certainties that tease, and squeeze.
They answer themselves with authority,
Their eyes at ease, while I stretch to see.

Revealed within the forest,
To the edges of the sea
Crowning glories all point to
That Grandest Mystery.

Less Fuzz, More Fizz

Slowing some,
Losing fizz,
Fighting "was"
To stay an "is".

Retreads to the Woodshed

Good times they're not deductin'
From the life span you're stuck in.
So try to re–tire when you retire
With brand new wheels to keep on truckin'.

Today is Not Tomorrow

Today is not tomorrow,
Tomorrow is not today.
So dissolve into the miracle,
The wonder and the lyrical,
Paddling those small thoughts away.

STAYING TOPSIDE

"Ugh. glug,
Who pulled the plug?"

"Over here.
C'mon. Steer."

LEARNING SAFETY

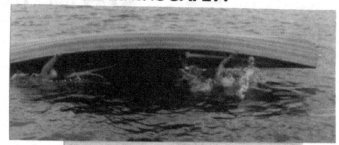

A nicely
planned
Oops!

"BE PREPARED"

"Hey – we're
not moving
very well
here."

"BETTER NOW
THAN LATER"

Accidents
May
Happen.
Tragedies
Needn't.

"PRACTICE
MAKES
PERFECT"

No No's

Would you wish to glean a sip
If you had to lean a bit,
And tipped?

Make Mine Water

The lake became rippled as he nipped
Then with whitecaps stippled; still he sipped.
Between gusts he tippled 'til, by urgency gripped,
With his reflexes crippled...he flipped.

They've found drowned paddlers
With open fly;
Not too hard to figure why.

Although a proper head
He may lack,
Passing motorists
Wave right back.
Tied up safely and with
Hardly a breeze
Even pumpkin heads wear
Their PFD's.

Whether on me or under
The seat under me,
I never go out
Minus my PFD.

An Old Bag in the Bow

No rocks for bow ballast,
Just water bag fill.
It levels on tilt.
It floats in a spill.

No foam for flotation,
Just water bag empty.
It takes lots less space,
And folds away neatly.

That old bag in the bow
Grants a trim safer run.
But truthfully, dear,
You're much more fun.

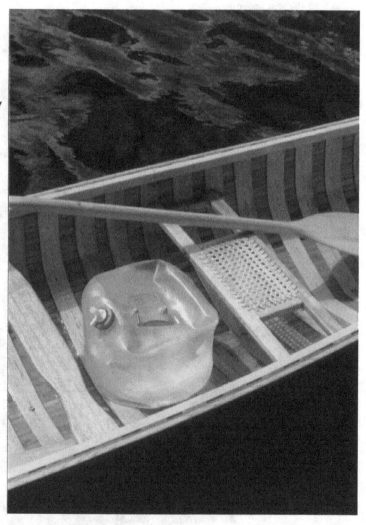

Leaves of Glass

He was 55
Had a few hours
Flew in for the day.

She was 5
Been out for a week
Portaged here with her Daddy.

He was also
Husband and father
Boss of his business
Knew all he had to.....
Man of the world.

She, full of faith
Still had things to learn
Took joy in them
As did others in her.

He fished
    Finished his bottle
        Smashed it against the rocks
            Flew out his catch
                Spoke of the bush with a touch of macho
                But mostly delight.

She swam
    Opened her foot on his bottle
        Was carried down the portage by Daddy
            Paddled home, rode to the hospital
                Wondering what kind of person
                    Would come all this way to the wilderness
                    Then mess it up.

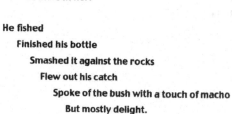

Winds might call
For a turnaround.
But turns poorly timed
Can send you

Down.

Robbie

Young Robbie, posted to Alaska,
Studied Aleut kayaks, then built one,
Carefully crafted from traditional materials.
He paddled the coast.

One day his craft sprung a leak,
Just as strong winds shifted to offshore
While the fog closed in.
Icy waters sealed his last option.

It was before wet suits and dry suits,
Airbags, inflatable PFD's,
Satellite tracking, GPS,
Cell phones, flares, built-in pumps,
And today's encouragements of backup and partnering.

Robbie was robust,
Knowledgeable, experienced, skilled.....
It wasn't enough.
Today's options for survival....
Too late for Robbie....
There for us.

OUT & BEYOND

Western Maryland has become a whitewater hot spot. The rivers of Maryland's Eastern Shore, for most of their history unconnected with the eastern seaboard, are an easy day's drive from New England and just hours away from the heavily populated New York to Washington megalopolis. Yet this bygone, bypassed, crabs-and-creeks country, between the busy sailing waters of the Chesapeake Bay and the magnetic draw of Atlantic beaches, continues largely undisturbed.

Michener's <u>Chesapeake</u>, overflowing with Shore history, natural and human, is one of the better known invitations to test these waters. There's a feeling of intimacy with nature as it was, and life in an earlier time. Many who make their living from the water do so in traditional craft, mostly of wood. Anything resembling a sea kayak easily becomes an "ice breaker".

You can ride currents and tides to the sea, or if you seek challenge, try your muscles and skills upriver against current, wind and tide.

Typically, no matter which larger river you pick, in just a few days you get to know an entire ecosystem.

The traditional river paddle, headwaters to mouth, camping on shore all along the way down is a possible adventure, no problem. But here you can also paddle an entire river, perhaps in up (or down) and back bites, in daily forays from a centrally located Maryland State Park campsite.

279

CHESAPEAKE RIVERS

In the Parking Lot of Dreams

Paddling upriver
On a zippity–doo–dah day,
I round the bend and run into....
One more abandoned floating city
Of swinging masts and flying bridges....
Another parking lot of mostly dreams.

There are no greetings; no one is here.
Boat owners, all elsewhere, and hard by the daily hustle.
Bobbing past in my "boat-lite"
I'm dwarfed by the impressive bows.
While buoyed by the aliveness of doing,
I'm sad for the ghost skippers and crews
Who work, earn and dream far from here.

Maybe because I'm closer to the water,
The shiny white fleet looks
Like, well,
A boneyard of headaches.
Everyone's "messing about" differs. "Boating is nonaligned,"
But this reaffirms my preference for boating unrefined.

So here's my little hum along...
To the water inclined,
Leaving shore things behind
I sure don't come out here
New problems to find.

When I break from the grind
To unbend and unwind
It's for boating that's kind
To my peace of mind.

Each stroke of the paddle
Past those craft that I'm "dissing"

Adds to the litany
Of just what I'm missing.

No docking or moorage,
No hauling or storage,
Ordinances, insurances,
Maintenance, appearances.

Painting, polishing, scraping, registrations,
Parking, security, launching, regulations,

Fueling, tuning, overhauling,
Analysis paralysis, the bank is calling,

Hourly workmen waiting for parts,
Subpoenas, marinas run by upstarts,

Blisters, blips, bleeps, and bubbles,
Pings and pitch-a-cup engine troubles,

Loans, credits, down-payment minimums,
Licenses, taxes, dues, dockominiums,

Parking hassles, sudden storms,
Numerous serpentine government forms,

Close calls and frights, another repair,
Sleepless rough nights, bills everywhere,

Coast guard boardings, oh woe is me,
Drug-dealing pirates, disasters at sea,

Or just palpitations, litigations,
Repossessions, liquidations...

Seized by the compulsion
To promote liberation
Paddling on I dispense
This thought for salvation:

"Lo, let it ensue without further ado;
You too can again become well-to-do ---
Just open the pit cocks, pay off the crew
And get you a nice new true-blue canoe."

Around the next bend the river narrows,
Shoreline greens reemerge.... there's Bambi!

I stop paddling, serenely adrift
Beyond sloshing bilge pumps, the thumping of generators,
In stillness listening for
The flutter of butterflies.

Florida is a sea kayaking state, and its best season is just the opposite of the rest of us. But Florida's explosive growth has hardly touched its extensive web of inland rivers. Yes, you can paddle the Everglades, the 10,000 Islands, the Inland Waterways both east and west coasts. But don't overlook the crystal clear gentle running rivers emerging from springs, with their sandy bottoms and overhanging wild tropical vegetation...and wildlife. About that wildlife – Paddling with manatees is as much fun as paddling with whales. In the cooler months you've never seen more, and different kinds of, birds. Deer and feral pigs abound. And there are the alligators. Not to be feared, but taken seriously.

Gators are definitely on a northerner's mind when first paddling these tropical rivers. (That little bit of edge explains and hopefully excuses the following hum–de–dum whimseys.) How dangerous are they? Not to be confused with salt water crocodiles, alligators are not into paddlers. Dogs have on occasion disappeared, and we wouldn't suggest your infant freely play along certain waters' edges. My only heart–skipping moment was on rounding a sharp bend on the upper Myakka River, when a snoozing granddaddy, equally startled, thrust himself into the water and under my kayak. Can't be sure of his length, only his belly, which appeared to be three times the width of my boat. (This was within minutes of being confronted by a camouflaged rifle–pointing guy emerging from the bushes, who turned out to be the park superintendent gunning for drug smugglers. The rest of the day was fine.)

Small Log or Big Nose

Sooner or later
Trailing fingers or toes,
You'll cater
To the gator
Seeking lunch with his nose.

Gourmet Canoe

Party of two,
Single canoe.
Is a gator sandwich made of gator?
Or the likes of me and you?

Not Returnable

That cheap phony-looking
Walmart-type sun-bleached
Faded-gray plastic alligator
There by the tree....
Just winked at me.

Please Don't Feed the Animals

A day of gory glory
For this hoary gourmet,
If the alligator ate 'er
At the Everglades buffet.

Here, my dear, is the Everglades stroke:
Into the bottom your paddle you poke.
Or sweep some water under the boat,
Then paddle like hell while it's slightly afloat.

"Would you both, please,
Look at the SAME gator?"

"We are!"

FLORIDA

Baja, with its whales, and Costa Rica, for its rivers, enjoy well-deserved popularity. At this time the coastal and interior regions of Belize still offer accessible true wilderness experience. Being on an inland river for an entire otherworldly week, with absolutely no sign or sound of other human activity except historical artifact-strewn caves, and where you hack out your own campsite is almost an impossibly rare experience these days.

BELIZE

Indiana Joneses in Eco-Tour Vacationland – A Dyspeptic Epic

When bit by the bot you do not die,
But get to be host to its lively larvae.
When your hatch lifts off, taking wing on the breeze,
Friends and neighbors will know you've been to Belize.
Where welts are svelte...this year's in-destination....
Back home you go for that true vacation.

Indiana Joneses wannabes
Join the eco-tour scene for balmy Belize
Escapees from lands of major freeze
To a sunshine land that knows not a sneeze.
Buoyantly healthy and bright they've arrived,
Adventurers come to kayak....

    (Flip to sweaty departure-lounge bums
    Dragging muddy and smelly pack.
    Been here but two weeks
    And hesitate to linger
    Scratching in strange places and
    A thorn in my writing finger.)

The ladies were all easy; that is, on the eye.
The men were hard as nails.
Our leader led with humor wry,
We were fed (and loved) fritters of snails.
Kayaked and camped islands out at sea;
Then total wild forest immersion.
Milo and re-repacking from cay to key,
Our major (admitted) perversion.

Sailed soft tropical puffs,
Paddled wind and waves,
Found shards, bones and teeth in
Unvisited caves.

Lunched knee-high in water
In mangrove terrain,
Stilt and stick biffies,
Rapids, and rain.

An osprey's nest
Formed the top of our biffy,
And she'd spread her wide wings
Every time things looked iffy.

Pappy's hors d'oeuvres treat
For the fearless and shameless
Was the dripping raw meat
Of fresh conch penis.

Ate lobster and fish balls,
Coconut and papaya
Then dropped deep upcountry
In the rainforest of the Maya.

Pitched in wet jungle,
Riding rubber kayaks.
Treed howler monkeys,
Many fresh jaguar tracks.

Downriver grind and bump,
Lean back and wiggle,
Avoid portage or pump
So back thrust and wriggle.

Push-overs, push off-ers,
Thrust and parry....
Lift-overs, push-unders,
Avoiding a carry.

Jump-outers, jump back-inners,
Over-jump and splash.
Dunk, then rise to a log, and thump,
Sweetly smiling as you bash.

Choppers, hold-backers,
Bouncers, squeezers,
Scrapers with stickers,
Dangling like teasers.

Scooter starters, belly flops,
And occasionally we try
At serious machete stops
An accomplished draw and pry.

Fun–in–the–sun burn,
Scratches, barbs, coral cuts,
Bug bites and blisters,
Aching muscles, falling nuts.

Various nefarious malarious
(And dengue fever) skeeters,
Scorpions, spiders, sand fleas –
Ravenous flesh eaters,

In waters with a crocodile,
Not supposed to be here, but was all the while.
And behind Tom's tent, the fer de lance,
Most bothersome, though, red pissy ants.

But none of this mattered, we were jungle jocks,
Empowered with shots and pills.
Pay up and you too can earn
Masochistic thrills.

Strangely so
For we all had such fun.
Great to be doing....
And successfully done.

Now counting our red and black souvenir spots,
And scratching recurrent itches
(From all those unknown welcoming
Little sons of witches).

Saw those glittering palaces cruising at sea.
No sympathy wasted, no fuss,
Those sanitized souls in bland luxury,
Scarless wimps, not heroic like us.

The Inimitable Inside Passage

North America's Inside Passage, for hundreds of Pacific West Coast miles, Puget Sound to Skagway, remains one of the planet's most spectacular wild places. It is here that the great canoes, dugouts from giant cedars, held sway. And even the baidarkas, the skin boats of the Aleuts, traveled these waters south as far as today's San Francisco, in quest of the otter. Small wonder that modern kayaking blossomed in this compelling largely inaccessible region which is especially accessible to paddlers.

Launching options abound. There are U.S. and Canadian ferry systems serving the Gulf and San Juan Islands, and British Columbia ferries to numerous coastal locations, including west to the Queen Charlottes and east as far as Bell Canola. With car or as foot passengers, kayakers and their boats are welcomed. That goes as well for the Alaska Marine Highway, with ferry schedules to villages as well as towns. Scheduled coastal services in British Columbia include the *"Lady Rose"*, with convenient kayak rentals, and the *"Uchuck III"*, which lowers you in your kayak and gently raises you back on board with its "bosun's pallet". There are motherships, sailing charters with canoes and kayaks aboard, and out of Glacier Bay Cruises, Alaska, the *"Wilderness Adventurer"* with kayaks and the *"Wilderness Explorer"*, which is a kayaker drop-off and pickup service.

Paddling tidal waters with snow-covered peaks in uninhabited chunks of territory as large as Switzerland, with quiet coves under the gaze of weathered totem poles, with lush rainforest, waterfalls, glaciers, and with whales including humpbacks plus orca, dolphins, eagles and bears, this is kayak country as good as it gets.

Dream on, with lots of available information and options. An exploration anywhere in this gigantic wonderland is well worth the effort.

BROKEN ISLANDS

BROUGHTON ARCHIPELAGO

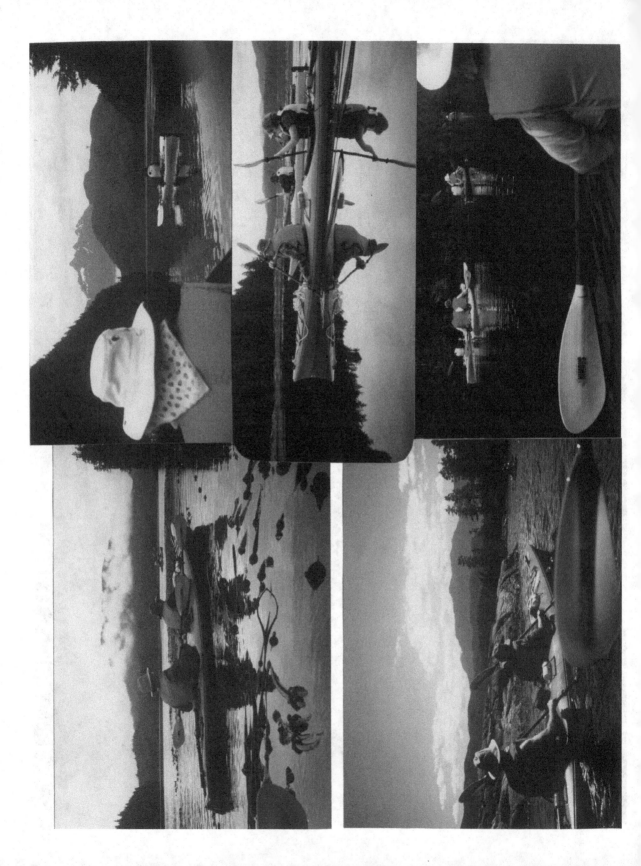

Malcolm Island Collectors

While orca play out in the bay
Our prey this day is rocks.
With irresistible patterns and shapes
And colors to knock off your socks.

Five fair-haired offspring of Finnish pioneers
Are drawn by the smell of the bannock,
Eyeing our rocks, they swing in the large
Beachcombed fishnet hammock.

Collecting stones is not in their bones.
"Why bother?" they ask, and we say,
"Cause they're pretty, and fun, and sparkle with sun."
And because we're from far away.

Later we saw them walking the beach
Scouting out everything once in their way.
Island kids laughing and filling the pails
Of parents too busy to play.

TOFINO/HOT SPRINGS/WEST COAST

GETTING STARTED.....
CLINICS

KYUQUOT SOUND

U 2 CAN CANOE – AND KAYAK TOO

LOTS

OF

FRIENDLY

HELP

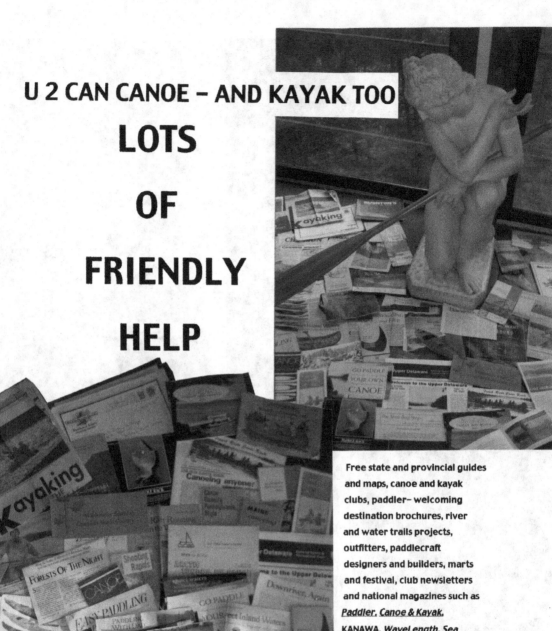

Free state and provincial guides and maps, canoe and kayak clubs, paddler– welcoming destination brochures, river and water trails projects, outfitters, paddlecraft designers and builders, marts and festival, club newsletters and national magazines such as *Paddler*, *Canoe & Kayak*, KANAWA, *WaveLength*, *Sea Kayaker*, free on–the–water tryouts and clinics, eco–tours, the American Canoe Association, PADDLE CANADA, and ...don't forget the Internet.

TRY & BUY

(Try *BEFORE* you buy)

Anthony Island Sentinels

Like the Haida,
And in a craft not unlike their own,
We dig deep our paddles until
The surge lifts us over
Kelp, rocks, starfish
Into this protected still lagoon.

Eight hundred people once
Carved canoes, fished, hunted,
Made war, and love, here in Ninstints.

Grounding gently, along a half-moon sweep of beach
We step softly into the presence of the spirits.
Weathered moss-covered figures return our stares.

Deer continue their nibbling at the feet of
These ancient totems, standing in a row still,
The logs of their homes returned to earth.

Bleached carvings, a beaver, bear, whale,
Each crest proclaiming witness
To bands and families disappeared, drifted into history.

Outside, beyond the cove and the cedars,
The Pacific's insistent surf
Is but a muffled sigh.

GLACIER BAY

How to Start a Town

No chunks of cobalt blue,
No aquamarine hue,
No double-bladed paddle,
No sleek new canoe.

Just frigid dark water
Facing Glacier Bay
On Icy Strait
That cold water day.

"Take a line ashore,"
Was the fishbuyer's need,
To anchor and store
With less caution than speed.

So a "cheechocker" deckhand,
Who of paddling knew,
Dropped into a fish box
In lieu of canoe.

In creaking salmon crate,
Leaking shocks through wood slats,
He kneeled prayerfully low
And paddled like bats.

Sinking; then grounding;
The line was ashore,
Hand and business saved
By a busted oar.

No glory, no cheers,
No heroic hue;
Just another fish day
In a square-bowed canoe.

Fifty years later
Returned to this cove,
Found a town with
A zip code, by Jove.

Update

The brothers on this side?
"Took some heavy seas going into Icy Strait,
Doused their engine,
Got blown to shore.
The youngest was found three days later,
Frozen across the top of a rock.
But he survived.....lost both legs,
Wheeled around town for years afterward."

Folks on the other side?
"Whole family, end of the season, October,
Headed for Juneau for winter supplies.
Got a blast of wind out of Glacier Bay.
Blew them over, everyone lost."

A Beachcomber's Gifts from the Sea

"Home run!" (Numerous softballs)

"Go!" (Dog-toothed tennis balls)

"Damn!" (Fishing lures)

"Fore!" (Golf balls off mega yachts)

"#^+@#^+!" (Glass floats from Asia)

"Mommy!" (Plastic boats, action figures, dolls)

"Yikes!" (Kayaker's light stick)

"Hi!" (Hand-carved Haida design in float, more than a decade at sea)

"Splash!" (Discarded homemade wooden woodpecker door knocker looking for a happier home)

"We're history,   (Hand-hewn nails, hand-blown bottle bottoms and

    Enjoy your day!"   every lovely empty shell)

U 2 CAN CANOE – AND KAYAK TOO

LOTS

OF

FRIENDLY

HELP

Free state and provincial guides and maps, canoe and kayak clubs, paddler– welcoming destination brochures, river and water trails projects, outfitters, paddlecraft designers and builders, marts and festival, club newsletters and national magazines such as *Paddler, Canoe & Kayak, KANAWA, WaveLength, Sea Kayaker,* free on–the–water tryouts and clinics, eco-tours, the American Canoe Association, PADDLE CANADA, and ...don't forget the Internet.

GETTING STARTED.....
CLINICS

**GUIDED
INSTRUCTION**

JOIN

A

CLUB?

TRY & BUY

(Try *BEFORE* you buy)

CRUISE
WITH A
GROUP

a/o
KISS OFF!

About the Author

Herb Klinger, a former Non-Western Studies teacher, canoeing counselor and tripping director, Camping and Guidance instructor at Teachers College, Columbia University, and the Recreation Chief of the US Job Corps, has been a lifelong paddler. Following travels in over a hundred and twenty countries and the publication of Knapsacking Abroad (Stackpole Books) and several best-selling color-sound filmstrip and video series including Man: A Cross-Cultural Approach, Global Cultures and Man: An Ecological Approach (Educational Design, Inc.), Herb's avocational interest in canoeing and kayaking became a major focus. He and his wife Judy spend much of their time on the British Columbia coast and paddling from an island cabin in Temagami, Ontario. His work has appeared in Anorak, Canoesport, Canoe & Kayak, Messing About in Boats, Sports Afield and Paddler.